...*And* THERE WAS A CALM

A MEMOIR

MARK WELLS
with Daniel K. Brantley

ARGYLE FOX
PUBLISHING

Table of Contents

*Dedicated to
my brothers & sisters in Christ,
who give me encouragement to keep
fighting the devil, hoping for the coming of Jesus,
and striving to be more like our Savior.*

. . . *And* THERE WAS A CALM

Man that is born of a woman is of few days and full of trouble.

—*Job 14:1*

Chapter 1

Can We Join You?

It was a stupid question. I see that now. At the time, it wasn't so clear.

My head and heart were at their emotional limits, thanks to a year of snowballing stress. I needed to get away, to vacate the premises of ordinary life, to regain some sanity and prepare myself for whatever came next.

———

I answered the phone. My wife, Stacy, was on the other end of the line, and she was frantic. With no explanation, she insisted I come home immediately.

"What's going on?" I asked.

"I'll tell you when you get here," she said. "Just get home."

Fearing the worst, I left work and burned rubber.

I burst through the front door, and Stacy explained

that she caught her teenage son—my youngest stepson, Travis—having sex with a neighbor girl. We didn't know Travis even liked the neighbor girl. The idea that he would have premarital sex with her—or anyone—never crossed our minds. Such behavior wasn't condoned in our Christian home. It was discouraged.

I reeled and tried to process the situation, to determine an appropriate response. Travis didn't make it easy on me—didn't give me time to think. He just unloaded a litany of bombs, one after another.

"This isn't the first time I've had sex," he said.

I searched my brain for words. They were there, but none of them fit together. When I finally untangled my tongue and pieced together a sentence, it was simple. I asked Travis when he first had sex.

"I was twelve." He didn't flinch. Acted like he was reporting the day's weather, not dropping a life-shattering explosive on his mother and me.

I got along well with Travis and his older brother, Matthew. We had a good relationship. I took the boys fishing and hunting. They played on the church softball team I coached. Sure, Stacy and I had to spend a couple days deprogramming the boys and getting rid of the smell of cigarettes, marijuana, and alcohol every other weekend after they visited their father, but that wasn't the boys' fault. That was on their dad. Travis and Matthew were good kids. I never imagined either of them would sneak around to have sex. Especially Travis. We trusted him.

Yet, somehow this happened right under my nose, and he'd been at it since he was twelve. I couldn't fathom how many signs I must have ignored. Because there are always signs, right? And I missed every one of them.

"That's not all," Travis said, relaxing on a kitchen stool.

He was playing a solo game of one-upmanship to see how much I could take. But I'd already gone well past my mental and emotional limits. Travis didn't care. He was done keeping secrets. Unloading was freeing, and he wanted more of that freedom.

"She's pregnant."

Somehow, my heart found room to sink deeper. My jaw dropped. I crossed my arms and stood beside Stacy, my knees threatening to give way. Neither of us spoke, stunned to silence by Travis's casual report.

"And one more thing." Travis's nonchalance paired perfectly with his year-round uniform of shorts and a T-shirt.

I didn't want to hear it, but Travis—this high school senior who was drunk on the power he suddenly wielded over the emotional well-being of his mother and me—was relentless.

"I think I have an STD."

"You know"—I magically found my voice—"you know you can die from those?"

Thankfully, Travis didn't have an STD. And while my revelation that STDs can be deadly didn't have its intended effect, another revelation did. Soon after Travis unloaded on Stacy and me, the young lady Travis impregnated had her own confession. She didn't know who the father was.

When the baby arrived a few months later, hospital staff swabbed Travis and the newborn for a DNA test.

Travis was indeed the father. The test proved it. If they'd just waited a couple days, I could have told them that, no lab test needed. The baby looked just like Travis.

A lab-confirmed father, Travis moved in with his girlfriend and her father and grandmother. Travis was committed to caring for his unexpected family, and Stacy and I wholeheartedly supported him. He was doing the right thing, and we followed suit. What choice did we have? We loved Travis, and as soon as we met baby Jaden, we fell in love with him also. We were powerless against his chubby cheeks and lack of dexterity.

So, Stacy and I bent over backward and did whatever we could to help Travis and his girlfriend during their first few months as parents. We bought them food, clothing, diapers, and a little red wagon. We babysat whenever they asked.

Life was different, but it was good. We were all learning our new roles, and Stacy and I fell into grandparenting with gusto.

Travis and his girlfriend lived a few houses away, and Travis often sat Jaden in the red wagon we bought them and carted Jaden over for a visit. Our hearts swelled anytime we looked outside and saw Travis pulling the wagon down the street toward our house.

Gradually, the shock of Travis's sexual revelations wore off, and a calm fell over that part of life.

———

The same time Travis was starting his new life as a parent, I got hooked on a new startup ministry. CATCH—Christian Anglers Together Can Help—targeted people who society generally ignored: young kids, older adults, and alcohol and drug addicts. We used fishing as a means for luring people in to hear the Gospel.

It was the only ministry I engaged in that took the Gospel beyond the four walls of the church building and met people where they were. Even in the ministry's infancy, it produced fruit. People were being saved. Between twenty-five and fifty kids gave their lives to the Lord at a single event, and we were just getting started.

Eager to grow the ministry and see God continue to work, the Board of Directors decided it would be beneficial to earn 501(c)(3) status. As Chairman of the Board, I was tasked with jumping through the legal hoops to make it happen.

Pouring myself into CATCH forced my hand and brought me face to face with my limitations. I had a choice to make: forge ahead with CATCH or maintain my position as a long-time Sunday school teacher.

The choice wasn't easy. I'd been teaching Sunday school at Clingan Ridge Baptist Church since Stacy and I married nearly a dozen years earlier in 1997. Initially, I cotaught the class, but I'd been teaching solo for eight years running. The class slowly, methodically worked through various books in the Bible, starting a new book every quarter.

However, teaching required a lot of time. While my friends were on the lake or in the woods, I was at home, studying and preparing for the week's lesson. It was a challenge, and the challenges didn't end outside the classroom door. They met me in the classroom.

One week, I admitted I didn't know what a passage meant. Multiple Bible commentators mentioned various interpretations that could be true, and no commentator held one interpretation as true over all others. Like them, I couldn't choose one interpretation over the other. Each had merit and seemed biblically sound. When I mentioned that in class, my mother-in-law raised her hand. "If you studied the Bible more," she said, "it will tell you what it means."

She wasn't joking, and the comment hurt. I was dumbfounded.

Stacy consoled me afterward. That evening, she called her mom and explained that faithful believers have disagreed on that specific passage for years. "Calling Mark out like that was uncalled for," she said. "Don't do it again. He puts a lot of effort into that class."

I don't remember how her mom replied, but I'd never been prouder of my wife.

Fortunately, such in-class drama was rare. Most weeks, class was pure joy, an opportunity to dig into God's word and grow in faith and understanding. We covered nearly every book during my tenure, from Genesis to Revelation, with help from resources produced by Lifeway Books. I loved the people who attended class and relished time with them each week.

If there were more hours in the day, I would have kept at it forever. But we only get twenty-four hours every day, and there wasn't enough time for teaching and CATCHing.

After much thought and prayer, I stepped down from my teaching position. It was necessary in order to give myself more fully to CATCH. While necessary, giving up that class felt like a death, and like every death, it required grieving.

———————

My grieving was compounded by life at home. At the same time I walked away from teaching Sunday school, Matthew—Stacy's oldest son—ran off.

He'd taken off before, but this was different. Usually, he only left for a few days at a time. Then he would show up at the front door like a stray cat looking for a bite to eat. Or he would call and ask us to pick him up, sometimes at his dad's place across town. Other times, we found him at the local homeless shelter or underneath the Mouse Creek bridge. After his dad moved to the South Carolina border, Matthew trekked all the way there and called us for a ride home.

Whenever Matthew returned, he never talked about why he ran off or what he was doing living under a bridge or at his dad's place. He just slinked back and bided his time until he left again.

His preference for street living confounded us. Our home was always open to him—our kitchen pantry full of food, bedrooms complete with comfortable bedding, and bathrooms featuring hot water. We loved Matthew and wanted the best for him, but he bristled at our care.

When we didn't hear from him for months, we feared the worst. We didn't know if he was near or far, dead or alive. He was missing in action when Jaden was born. He was gone when Travis broke up with his girlfriend. And when Travis's ex-girlfriend forbade us from seeing Jaden, Matthew was nowhere to be found.

———————

On September 10, 2009, Matthew was missing, Travis was struggling with his responsibilities as a young father, my Sunday school class was no longer my Sunday school class, and three months had passed since Stacy and I last saw our grandson. Everywhere I looked, I saw brokenness and heartache.

My marriage was the one area of life that felt healthy. We'd been through a lot, but Stacy and I clung to one another and squeezed our Savior tight. Still, the external stresses threatened to undo me.

I was at a breaking point when I arrived at a local farm in western Bradley County. The farmer wanted some catfish removed from his pond, so CATCH gathered up some alcoholics and drug addicts to lend a hand. For a few hours, that group of men and women who struggled with substance abuse disorders were at peace. They weren't stressed about court dates or mandatory counseling sessions. No one complained about the pull addiction had on them and the struggle to stay clean. All they cared about was yanking another catfish out of the pond.

Near the middle of the day, Stacy and I headed to the CATCH trailer for something to eat. As we neared the trailer, Jerri McCleese and her daughter, Leslie, pulled over on the side of Bigsby Creek Road. They lived just down the street and wondered what we were doing in their neck of the woods. I explained and asked about Jerri's husband, Chris.

"Oh, he's just getting off work," Jerri said. "He'll be coming through soon."

A few minutes later, Chris was leaning against the CATCH trailer, telling me about his upcoming family vacation. They were heading to Savannah, Georgia, the same place Stacy and I honeymooned after ten years of marriage.*

At the time, Chris was Manager of the local Walmart that gave a sizable donation of cash and food to support CATCH kid events. We met a couple months earlier, but I hardly knew him. We never spent time together in the real world, away from the ministry. But I didn't let that stop me.

I needed a vacation, some time to clear my head and leave all the stresses behind. I needed a few days in Savannah to be concerned about nothing more than reapplying sunscreen and finding a good restaurant for dinner.

---

* *I know—ten years is a long time to wait for a honeymoon. But better late than never, right?*

That's why I asked the question—that stupid question I never asked before and hereby vow to never ask again, no matter what.

"Chris," I said, my eyes locked on his, "can we join you?"

Chapter 2

Traveling by Automobile, Boat & Air

THE QUESTION SURPRISED STACY. IT was a little presumptive for her taste. But her desire to get away to Savannah outweighed any reservations she had. So, she didn't make a big stink when I asked a recently acquired acquaintance if my wife and I could butt in on his family vacation.

Chris wasn't bothered at all. He didn't skip a beat or consult his wife, Jerri. He just laughed.

"Really?" he said. "Of course! It'll be great. The more the merrier!"

Like that, Stacy and I were set to hijack the McCleese family vacation to Savannah. It was that easy.

The following Thursday evening, we pulled up to Chris and Jerri's house. Joining us were Chris's father-in-law, Doug, and a couple we'd not met, Carl and Tai. After some quick handshakes and navigation talk, we loaded up and hit the road, a three-car caravan carrying half a dozen people who were ready to put the stresses of everyday life in the rearview mirror.

Six hours of driving and a quick dinner stop at Cracker Barrel later, we reached our three-story rental house in Savannah. It was early Friday morning. We stumbled out of the car and stretched, banged out a few quick games of ping-pong in the basement, wandered to our respective bedrooms, and passed out.

A few hours later, the house came to life. Fueled by coffee and a need to venture out, we climbed back into our cars and drove to River Street Marketplace, an open-air riverfront market.

We weaved in and out of shops, drunk on the salty air and the smell of fresh seafood. Inspired by the sights and smells, one of the men suggested we leave the ladies to their shopping and go catch our own fresh seafood. No one had to convince me. All we needed was a guide to get us on the water, and I'd make sure we had plenty to eat.

Despite being in a coastal city, finding a legitimate guide took some work. Guide advertisements littered the town, but they all fell flat. Every address put us in front of a random house with no indication that a business existed inside. Since none of us wanted to beat on a stranger's door and risk having a serial killer await our arrival, we headed to a local marina in search of a better choice.

There, a scrawny, sun-browned guy made a couple calls and connected us with a deep-sea guide. We booked an eight-hour trip for the next morning, and I spent the rest of the day dreaming about all the fish I would land. It would be my first time fishing in salt water, and I was eager to put my mark on the Atlantic Ocean.

———————

The sun was shining on a different hemisphere when I kissed Stacy goodbye and told her I loved her. I settled into the car with Chris, Doug, and Carl and nibbled on a tiny box of raisins.

Chris pointed at my bite-sized breakfast as we drove toward our destiny. "You're gonna get the scours," he joked.

I tossed another raisin in my mouth and grinned as the car turned the corner. A few minutes later, we rolled up to Bull River Marina. It was nearly six o'clock, and the captain was already there. He introduced himself as Tommy and told us to hang out while he readied the boat for our excursion.

"We're gonna catch a lot of fish today," he promised.

He didn't have to tell me that. I was a fishing machine. Of course I would catch a lot of fish.

Chris, Doug, Carl, and I stood around, pointing out features of docked boats and dreaming of the coming adventure. Captain Tommy grunted as he heaved gear into his triple-hull, twenty-eight-foot catamaran, Nauti Dawg. Once the boat was loaded up, Captain Tommy launched into his obligatory safety talk.

"We've got life jackets for everyone," our shirtless,

big-boned guide said. "You don't have to wear them, but they're available if you want them."

I tuned out the rest. My imagination was too busy to leave room for safety instructions. What would tug on the end of my fishing line—tuna, snapper, or grouper? Maybe a shark or swordfish? The options were as limitless as the ocean. But even the ocean's offerings couldn't outdo my imagination.

Hope fully engaged, I climbed onto the Nauti Dawg and took a seat on the boat's bow. Chris and Doug flanked me, the three of us facing Carl, whose seat pointed forward and was situated near the captain. The first mate untied the boat from the dock, the captain started the boat's twin 250-horsepower motors, and we motored away.

The top of Bull River was glass, the only disturbances to the surface caused by our boat. Grasses pushed through the water on either side of the river, providing the perfect hiding place for skittish bait fish. Tall white ibis—elegant creatures I'd never seen before—stood frozen in place as they stalked prey in the marshy habitat. Over my shoulder, the sun peeked above the horizon, spraying the sky with an array of oranges, blues, and purples that would make Thomas Kincade, self-described "Painter of Light," blush.

Over the years, I did a lot of fishing. Countless weekends were spent cruising the Chickamauga Lake in my twenty-foot Ranger bass boat with the family, hunting large and smallmouth bass. When I wasn't fishing with Stacy and the boys, I was tournament fishing with my brother and brother-in-law at Nickajack Lake and Watts Bar Lake.

I saw a lot of beauty on those trips. But bass fishing in Tennessee didn't prepare me for this. That morning on the East Coast was something else, something worth writing home about and putting in a scrapbook to remember forever.

I inhaled deeply, relishing the wind and water spray. I considered the blessings of my good God. I was on vacation in a beautiful place, seeing beautiful things, heading out with great people for an unforgettable day of deep-sea fishing. I felt like a kid in a candy store.

I thought, "God must really love us to give us such a wonderful playground."

He did love us. Still does. Always will.

We were nearly out of Bull River when the boat coasted to a near stop. The twin motors idled. Behind me, the river estuary opened up to the Atlantic Ocean. We all eyed Captain Tommy.

"We're about to get into the ocean," he said, "and I want you to know, we're going to catch a lot of fish."

It was the second time he said it, and it meant more with the repetition. I wanted to shout for joy, but I held it together.

Captain Tommy put the boat in gear, cranked the stereo, and steered toward the Gulf Stream, where he insisted we would find fish. As we transitioned from the glassy Bull River to the choppy Atlantic Ocean, Bob Marley blasted through the speakers, encouraging us to not worry, that everything would be fine. There was no reason to disagree—not on a day like this.

In less than half an hour, land was just a memory. We

were surrounded by water on every side and making our way to meet the myriad fish that would soon fill the Nauti Dawg's cooler.

This wasn't the first time I was too far from the shore to see it. A few years earlier, I was in a similar situation. Miles from land, I laughed, ate, and lounged on a cruise boat with thousands of strangers. Even on that gigantic cruise ship, the ocean's vastness took my breath away, its size unveiling my smallness in new ways. This time, I felt my miniature size in a new way. Surrounded by the rough ocean waters, the twenty-eight-foot Nauti Dawg—an impressive watercraft when skipping through marshy river water—became little more than a grain of sand, a grain of sand that dwarfed me.

Thankfully, God cares about small things.

The waves picked up. One hit the hull hard and lifted Chris and me out of our seats. Chris didn't hesitate. As soon as he landed, he made a wobbly beeline to an open seat beside Carl.

I raised a questioning eyebrow.

Chris leaned toward me from the comfort of his new seat. "It's a smoother ride on this side," he yelled.

I nodded, wishing I took the seat before Chris thought of it. It indeed looked like a smoother ride. Added perk: It faced the right direction, allowing Chris to see where we were going. It was unnerving to ride backward on the Nauti Dawg, slamming into wave after wave, never knowing what was coming next. But I was too slow. I missed my opportunity for a smoother ride. Now, the seat of comfort and smooth riding belonged to Chris. I would have to tough it out on the backward-facing bow seat.

I later learned there were more seats behind the captain, but they were folded down, so I didn't know they were available. Had I seen them, I may have taken one of them. Maybe not though. I may have stayed put and just taken the waves' abuse. After all, the captain didn't seem concerned. He never announced that we were approaching rough waves or recommended we take special precaution. In fact, he took the opposite tact.

Intending to power through the growing waves, Captain Tommy opened up the throttle. The engines roared in response, sending the boat into the next wave at full speed.

Then, I went airborne.

Chapter 3

When Friends Care, They Slap You

I DIDN'T FLAIL AROUND IN the air, scrambling to grab hold of the boat that was somewhere underneath me. I didn't fear landing in the ocean and getting swallowed by a giant fish, torn apart by a great white, or buried under crashing waves. I just shot up in the seated position. But I wasn't the only thing in the air. So was the Nauti Dawg.

Its twin motors, which propelled us forward only moments earlier, were rendered useless. They screamed above the water's surface, choking on air, threatening to become permanently disabled. But the engines' scream didn't last long. Another wave slammed into the boat's hull, rescuing the engines from certain death and thrusting the boat upward. That's when I made my dramatic return.

The impact of those conflicting forces—my body falling from the sky and the boat rising in anger—focused on my spine. I slammed onto my seat and tumbled off, landing on top of Doug, who was face down on the boat deck, clambering to get up—a task made significantly more difficult with me flopping on top of him like a fish out of water.

With the boat rocking underneath me, I pushed off Doug with both of my hands and clawed my way back to my seat. But something was wrong. My legs didn't come with me. I looked down. They were attached to my body, but for one bizarre moment, I couldn't feel them. They were dead to me—present but absent at the same time. Then, the pain set in.

I screamed in agony. My legs were on fire, engulfed in invisible flames.

I wasn't the only one in pain. Doug, twenty years my senior, held his back and winced. He was hurt—and my landing on him didn't help any, but his legs weren't on fire. Mine were.

Not sure what else to do, I screamed—a lot. Between screams, I listened to the others talk.

"It's just a temporary stinger," one of them said. "It won't last long."

"He'll snap out of it," insisted another.

"We're still going fishing, right?"

"Don't want to cancel the trip."

"Yeah, Mark'll be fine."

I hoped they were right—that it was just a stinger, and the pain would subside in a few minutes. The flame coating the inside of my legs told me they were wrong.

Meanwhile, the sun poured through the cloudless sky

in an effort to match the internal heat my legs produced, highlighting the brilliant blue sky that served as the perfect backdrop for a day of pulling in one fish after another. I complemented the day's beauty with nonstop shrieking.

Thirty minutes into my screamfest, Carl took a step toward our indifferent captain. Normally reserved, quiet, and calm, Carl glared. His face hardened. "Call the Coast Guard!" he demanded.

Something in Carl's eyes or voice made the captain obey. Without a moment's hesitation, Captain Tommy phoned the Coast Guard, squashing any remaining hope that we would eventually continue our fishing excursion. This wasn't a stinger I could shake off, I wasn't going to be fine, and our fishing trip was over. My fishing dreams faded to the background, as pain took center stage.

Captain Tommy jawed with the Coast Guard as Chris laid me across the boat's bow and looked me over. There was no blood, no obvious sign of damage. But I didn't need signs. My legs burned like someone doused them in gasoline and lit them on fire.

"Chris," I shouted, "my legs—they're burning. Please, they're burning!"

Chris crossed the boat in search of something—anything—to dull the pain. He returned with his hands full of ice, ice intended to preserve the fish we were supposed to catch that day. He placed a chunk of the frozen stuff against my leg. In an instant, 1,000 needles pierced my skin.

"Take it off!" I gritted my teeth and swung my arms for emphasis.

Chris tossed the ice over the hull and held his head in his hands. The burning intensified. I wanted to die, confident that—as Scripture makes clear—death would bring an end to all suffering and a start to all joy. Paul's claim that "to live is Christ, to die is gain" rang true and called to me. I longed to experience that gain for myself, to escape this mortal coil.

Then, something slammed into my jaw—once, twice, three times. I opened my eyes. Chris stood over me, his open palm raised and ready. I lifted a hand to my cheek, the source of a new throbbing pain. "Are you slapping me?" I asked.

Chris didn't respond. He didn't have to. His raised hand and my hurting face provided all the answers I needed. The guy just slapped me, rapid-fire. I get it—I ruined the fishing trip with my burning legs. I should have grabbed one of those chairs behind the captain or clung to my seat when we hit that wave. But was this really my reward—a slap in the face?

"Don't close your eyes again." Chris's voice was unsteady. A tear threatened at the corner of one eye. He later explained that my accident made him relive his own past trauma from when an automobile accident sent him into shock and threatened his life. The only thing that saved him from death was maintaining consciousness, which required a friend to slap him incessantly. He was going to do the same for me, whether I wanted it or not. "You're scaring me, Mark," he said. "Don't close your eyes."

I wanted to keep my eyes open, but the sun was so

bright, and I was staring right at it. So, I closed my eyes and screamed in pain. As long as I made enough noise, Chris was content to not slap me. I kept it up.

Over the radio, Captain Tommy consulted with the Coast Guard, answering one question after another.

How old is he?

"Thirty-nine."

Height and weight?

"Six-foot-three, two hundred thirty."

Number of souls onboard?

"Six."

The ocean beat against the boat, sending shock waves of pain through my body.

Between screaming fits, I caught snippets of conversation between the captain and Coast Guard, but I didn't care what they said. I was too busy fighting my body's attempt to render itself unconscious. Despite my efforts, the pain was too much. Over and over, my burning legs overwhelmed me and knocked me out. Every time, I woke up to Chris frantically slapping my face. I learned a valuable, unexpected lesson that day: When friends care about you, even if they're casual friends you've only met a few times, they slap you.

Screaming, passing out, and waking up to slaps became my new routine. Then something caught my eye and quieted the burning in my legs.

Overhead, a monarch butterfly flapped across the expansive sky. Oblivious to the suffering and chaos on the Nauti Dawg, the butterfly rode the wind on its journey toward a distant shore I feared I would never see again.

"Chris," I said, motioning to the sky, "you see that butterfly?"

Chris craned his neck and looked up. The butterfly flitted against the blue sky above, making slow but measured progress. Chris turned back and shook his head. He didn't see it.

Disappointing, but no big deal. The butterfly was real, but it was hard to see—a shrinking speck of orange against an unending blue background. I wasn't hallucinating. I was sure of that. Well, pretty sure. There was a butterfly in the sky and I saw it, even if Christ didn't.

A jolt of pain shot through me as the butterfly distanced itself from the boat. *What was that thing doing so far from shore? How would it make it home?* The tiny flying critter got smaller by the moment, but it remained in focus, as clear and solid as Chris and our bare-bellied captain who continued his unharried radio chatter with the Coast Guard.

The butterfly was nearly out of sight, little more than a distant dot, when something else grabbed my attention. "I see them!" someone shouted. "I see them!"

The Coast Guard was near. I was going to live, and I wouldn't suffer another friendly slap from Chris. Or so it seemed.

Chapter 4

Rushing to Safety at 4 Knots

At the Coast Guard's direction, all Nauti Dawg passengers slipped into life vests. Except for me. I lay on the bow, dancing between screams and unconsciousness, unburdened by flotation devices.

Two Coast Guardsmen—one male, one female— boarded the boat. The female approached me. Her ponytail bounced from side to side as she took my blood pressure, pulse, and other vitals.

More waves. More screaming. "Where are we going?" I raised my head, my eyes slitted to block out the sun.

My Coast Guard assistant didn't know. So, I asked the question a dozen more times. Her answer didn't change. "We'll take good care of you," she promised. "We're doing our best."

The waves kept coming, giving me ample opportunity

to use my vocal chords to show the Coast Guardsmen how much I hurt.

"Are you going to fly me out of here on a helicopter?" I asked.

My Coast Guard attendant didn't know the answer to this question either. Or maybe she didn't want to break my heart. Helicopter rescues are reserved for people who are bleeding or get thrown overboard into the open ocean. I didn't know that at the time, and no one—not even my Coast Guard rescuers—told me. Had they shared this bit of news, I would have begged someone to cut me and toss me into the sea. If they refused, I would have grabbed a knife and slashed my burning legs, then dragged myself overboard. Anything to get off the Nauti Dawg and onto a helicopter. But I was ignorant at the time and unable to think of anything but the pain.

"Mark, Mark!" Someone screamed my name. The voice was clear but distant, coated in a haze of unconsciousness. "Mark, stay with us!"

I couldn't stay awake. The pain wouldn't let me. I was in and out of consciousness again. Waves—so many waves!

In moments when I was awake, I noticed Chris holding one of my hands. The female Coast Guardsman held the other, a thoughtful gesture that proved she, too, was at the limits of her abilities. All she could do now was hold my hand. I couldn't begrudge her lack of medical expertise. She trained to rescue people, not evaluate their health needs and treat them while riding angry Atlantic waves on a twenty-eight-foot boat captained by the bulbous-bellied Tommy. I was just thankful Chris hadn't slapped me since the Coast Guard arrived. It's the little things that matter.

Across the boat, Doug balanced gingerly on the edge of his seat, facing me and nursing his back. Much later, an X-ray discovered Doug broke his back. For now, all we knew was Doug was hurting, but he was in better shape than me.

Captain Tommy and the male Coast Guardsman reviewed the captain's licenses and paperwork. Then the captain turned the boat and started the trek back across the ocean at a whopping four knots per hour.* As we puttered toward the unseen shore, the male Coast Guardsman called emergency services in Savannah to ensure they were on hand and ready when we arrived.

I squinted and looked up. Something danced across my field of vision.

"Hey, Chris."

Chris squeezed my hand, which let me know I was conscious and my vocal cords still worked. "Yeah, buddy."

A second monarch butterfly floated overhead. The sun shone through its brown and black wings and body, as the creature made its way toward the safety of the distant shore. I took a quick breath. "Do you see that butterfly?"

Chris gave the sky a cursory glance, then frowned slightly. "No," he said, "I don't see it."

Another shock of pain moved through my legs, my agony exacerbated by the look Chris gave my hand-holding Coast Guard rescuer. "He's losing it," Chris said without opening his mouth or making a peep. The female

---

Four knots is approximately four and one-half miles per hour.

Coast Guardsman answered with an almost imperceptible head nod.

It didn't matter that Chris didn't see the butterfly. He didn't look long enough. It was there, and I saw it. Well, I thought I saw it.

More waves. More screaming.

Maybe Chris was right. Maybe I was losing my mind. Why would butterflies be so far from shore? It didn't make any sense. They couldn't survive out here, could they?**
The pain had done a job on me. This kind of trauma could make a man see things. Wouldn't be the first time.

A second Coast Guard vessel arrived to get in on the action. Chris and my attending Coast Guardsman released my hands to greet the newcomers. Without their support, the boat's rocking left me uneasy and unbalanced, so I reached overhead and grabbed the metal bar that wrapped around the bow. Holding the bar gave me a sense of stability and security—for a moment.

Before I could relax, enter another screaming fit, or pass out, the newly arrived vessel sidled up to the Nauti Dawg and brushed against its side, crushing my hand against the thin metal bar in the process. Fortunately, the burning raged in my legs, allowing my compressed hand to go practically unnoticed.

No one from the second Coast Guard boat boarded the Nauti Dawg. After a quick conversation with their colleagues and a complementary hand crushing for me,

---

**It sounds crazy, but I later learned that butterflies have been known to fly across the Atlantic Ocean.*

the second boat of Coast Guardsmen took the lead in our three-boat caravan.

With one boat in front and another behind to keep some waves off the Nauti Dawg, we could speed up and get to shore faster, and I would experience less pain and remain conscious for longer periods. That was the hope, at least. In reality, there was no noticeable difference. The ocean was too powerful. So, we chugged along at the same mind-numbing speed of four knots an hour, onward and into more waves, more pain, more screaming.

Another hour passed.

"Chris!" I yelled.

Chris pressed my hand with both of his.

I pointed up. "Do you see that butterfly—that one right there?" This time, I raised an arm. I pointed a finger at the butterfly and followed its path across the blindingly bright sky. "Tell me you see it, Chris! Do you see it?"

Chris covered his eyes against the sun and followed the path of my finger. "Yes!" he said, a half grin tugging at the corner of his mouth. "I see it—I do!"

I dropped my arm to my side in relief. Third time was a charm. The butterfly was real, and Chris saw it. I wasn't going crazy, and—equally good news—Chris wasn't as dense as I thought. He just needed a little direction.

We inched forward, fighting the churning ocean in slow motion. We'd been driving for three hours when

Chris said we had to be close to shore. If land was nearby, our cell phones might work.

"My wife!" I yelled. Stacy needed to know what happened. "Someone call my wife!"

Doug pulled out his phone and got Stacy on the line. She and the other ladies were still shopping. I ruined that also. With a single phone call, the ladies' shopping fun met the same fate as our men's fishing trip.

Another hour passed, and the boat finally sped up. We were back in river water. The Nauti Dawg skimmed its surface, Captain Tommy pushing his boat to keep pace with the lead Coast Guard watercraft that buzzed toward the marina. It wasn't the same marina we launched from that morning—Bull River Marina was too far away. We needed something closer, and this marina was it.

The next few moments were a flurry. Firefighters leapt onto the boat deck as the Nauti Dawg slid to a stop. The first mate went to work, securing the boat against the dock. Coast Guard members gave the firefighters a brief rundown of the situation, then exited the boat to inform other first responders on site. Ambulances, police cars, and fire trucks crowded the marina parking lot.

Careful not to worsen my injuries, the firefighters shuffled me onto a backboard and lifted me off the boat and onto the deck. I lay on my back, looking into the sun.

I yelled for my wife.

"I'm here!" Stacy shouted.

I didn't see her, but hearing her voice was enough. She was near, and her presence brought me a tinge of peace I'd not felt for four and a half hours.

That peace swelled when a strong pair of hands cupped my neck. "I have cervical secure." The voice attached to the hands had the authority of a firefighter. "I'm Tommy," he said, "Tommy Blackston. What's your name?"

I told him my name, and he—like the hand-holding Coast Guardsman from the boat—promised to take good care of me. With no waves sending pain shooting through my body, I believed Tommy.

I closed my eyes against the sun's brightness, comforted that I was in the cupped hands of an expert. When I did, I felt something I never wanted to feel again—a hand slapping my face.

My eyes popped open. An older gentleman wearing a marina security badge stood over me. His hand hung by his side. "Mark," he said, "stay with us."

"I'm fine!" I said, wondering how he knew my name and whether everyone around here had past trauma they needed to work out on my face. "I'm fine!"

I bit my tongue to hold back a few other choice words. After getting smacked around by a friend on the ocean, I was not eager to have a stranger continue the routine.

The sun focused its rays on my retinas, and I closed my eyes again for respite.

SMACK!

"Mark!" the security guard shouted as if his hand against my face wasn't enough to get my attention.

"I'm fi—"

"Buddy, you slap him one more time"—Tommy's face remained just out of view, and his voice boomed—"and you and I are gonna have problems."

The security guard withered under Tommy's warning and whimpered away with his tail between his legs. If I wasn't stuck on that backboard, I would have jumped to my feet and hugged Tommy. I would have added him to my will if he asked or given him my beloved bass boat. No price was too precious for the assurance that I wouldn't get slapped by another stranger or friend under Tommy's watch.

But I couldn't jump to my feet, and Tommy didn't mention becoming my heir. So, I closed my eyes and thanked God for small mercies. Then I thanked Tommy for saving me from the smack-happy senior security guard.

Soon, a group of first responders lifted me and the backboard from the ground. They moved carefully as firefighter Tommy kept my neck in place, but their caution wasn't enough. The slightest movement sent new pains through my body. I screamed all the way up the dock and to the ambulance. When the EMTs situated me inside the back of the ambulance, I shouted for Stacy.

"Yes, sweetheart," she said.

I still couldn't see her, but I needed her to know I loved her. I shouted it.

"I love you, too," Stacy called out.

The ambulance engine rumbled, ready to rush me to the nearest hospital. Stacy sat in the front seat beside the driver, and I lay in the back, attended by an EMT. Finally beyond the reach of the sun, I opened my eyes.

The ambulance thundered away from the marina, every bump in the road introducing me to a new pain.

"Stacy," I said, "you there?"

"I'm here, Mark."

"I love you, Stacy."

The ambulance's siren screamed. I screamed.

"I love you, Mark," Stacy replied.

Outside of the ambulance, marina employees stood sentry at intersections, blocking traffic to give us a straight, unencumbered shot to Memorial Hospital in Savannah. Despite their efforts, pedestrian automobiles made their way onto our path, driving alongside the ambulance on the way to whatever normalcy their days entailed. The ambulance driver shouted out the window for these oblivious drivers to get out of the way. My body tensed. Ambulance drivers deal with emergencies every day, but this guy seemed abnormally anxious. Was I the worst case he'd ever seen? Maybe not, but I was in bad enough shape to send a professional ambulance driver into road rage.

The driver buried the gas pedal and soon, we were at the hospital. The back door swung open and, in a flash, EMS handed me off to the hospital's trauma team. Hospital staff transferred me to a hospital gurney and sprinted with me toward the emergency entry.

Above, the world transitioned from ambulance roof to open sky to hospital entryway, and then—

It wasn't the work of an expert, but it wasn't created by a child either. A thick, black outline kept pinks, blues, and greens in their proper places. Above the colors, two thick lines served as antennae. My care team rushed me past the painting and toward whatever awaited me, leaving me with a silly question:

Why did someone paint a butterfly on the ceiling?

Chapter 5

All Hands on Deck

INSIDE MEMORIAL HOSPITAL'S TRAUMA DEPARTMENT, nurses and doctors surrounded my bed, their blue scrubs and white jackets swishing with urgency. They poked and prodded, pushed me this way and that, looking for signs of blood or misplaced bone.

Apparently, my clothes blocked the view of any potential injuries. So, a nurse cut off my swimsuit, laying everything bare on that cold gurney. My embarrassment, however, was short-lived. These people didn't care what was under my suit. They just wanted to help.

Convinced there was nothing to be ashamed about, I asked Stacy if she could fix the shorts when we got home. It wasn't a particularly nice swimsuit, but I paid for it and—well, I can squeeze a penny 'til it screams. I don't remember her answer. Since I never saw the suit again, it must have been *No*.

I showed off the screaming I'd perfected over the

previous five hours, but no one seemed to notice. They just looked me over, lifting my legs and twisting my arms, doubling their investigation as an interrogation.

"How old are you?"

"What's your name?"

"Do you know where you are?"

"What medications are you on?"

If they stopped moving me around, I could have given some answers. But they insisted on flipping me from one side to the other. In return, I spent all my energy wearing out my larynx without answering a single question.

Then, their questions and my screaming came to a sudden halt. The sedatives from the EMT finally kicked in, and the pain eased up a bit. I rolled my head to the left and right. Except for Stacy and me, the room was empty.

Stacy and I shared the sterile space, chatting in sporadic spurts. We spoke quietly, my throat and her ears enjoying the unexpected break. She sat by my bed, holding my hand and insisting we would make it to the other side. It was a genuine Hallmark moment, until my thirst interrupted. I'd been thirsty before, but not like this. My mouth was the Sahara Desert, and my body felt drained of all fluid.

"Can I get some water, please?" What would have usually been a calm request was a belligerent demand. I yelled the question to the small, empty trauma bay, hoping it would bounce out of the room and into the eardrum of someone who could fulfill my request.

A nurse rushed in. For some reason, her hands were empty—not even a Dixie cup of water. "Has the doctor not been back here yet?"

Stacy shook her head. We'd not seen a doctor or anyone else for nearly fifteen minutes. The nurse spun on her heels and left, ignoring my water request. A doctor entered soon after, a grim look plastered on his face. He motioned to Stacy, who followed him through a door to my left.

I lay alone on the gurney, curious whether I would ever taste water again or if my throat would dry up and wither away. I geared up to call for water again when Stacy returned to my side.

"The doctor," Stacy started, her lip quivering, "he said you're gonna be okay."

I cocked an eyebrow in doubt. Stacy attempted to maintain her composure, but her efforts were futile. She was going to fall apart. Her poker face betrayed the truth, and I needed to hear it from her.

"What did he really say?" I asked.

Stacy's body spasmed with grief. "He said your back is broken." She didn't even try to stop the tears. "Your spinal cord—it's cut."

The doctor didn't know how bad the damage was or how it would affect me. In fact, I never got an official prognosis that pinpointed what I should expect in the coming weeks, months, or years. All we knew was things didn't look good.

I didn't know what to say. Stacy did. She was an RN at the local nursing home in Cleveland, Tennessee, and she knew how to compartmentalize. She wiped away her tears, pushed aside her fears, and went into nurse mode.

"What do you want me to do?" she asked.

I thought about my damaged spinal cord with a sudden clarity and calmness. My mouth remained dry, aching for moisture, but whatever ingredients were in the pain meds worked well. I didn't feel the need to scream about my cotton mouth anymore. *Thank you, Lord, for pain medication.*

"Call the pastor and my parents," I said. "Tell them to start praying." I needed prayer warriors, people who could touch the hem of Jesus's garment on my behalf.

Thankful to have something to do, some task to complete, Stacy called my parents and Pastor Ricky Vaughn to fill them in on what happened.

After Stacy hung up with my parents and pastor, the doctor returned. His white hair bounced on his head. "I'm Dr. Cannon, and I'll be doing your surgery tomorrow," he said. "My son-in-law is also a surgeon. He'll open you up so I can see your spine, then I'll do the procedure."

He explained that when I landed on the boat, my twelfth thoracic vertebrae (T12) shattered, a break known as a T12 burst fracture. According to Dr. Cannon, it was an incomplete spinal cord injury, so I might retain some feeling below my waist. If I did, Dr. Cannon couldn't guarantee or even guess what feeling that might include.

Dr. Cannon explained that his son-in-law would cut me down the side, from my armpit to the middle of my stomach, then pull out my guts to give a clear view of my spine. Once my guts were on a bedside table, Dr. Cannon would go to work. He planned to install a titanium cage around the vertebral bones above and below my damaged T12. Two screws in top and two in bottom would hold the cage in place. Once installed, the cage would stabilize my spine, reducing my pain and leading me one step toward a future recovery.

Despite hearing that my guts would be placed on a sterile table within the next twenty-four hours, I was at ease. I trusted Dr. Cannon. Trust was the only response I could muster. I was maxed out on the amount of information I could retain, and I didn't have the energy to think of any questions. The drugs running through my veins made sure of that.

———————

Whatever Stacy told my parents on the phone had its intended effect.

My younger brother, Jamie, sped from Chattanooga to Cleveland to pick up my parents and older sister, Lisa. Mom wanted to fly to Savannah, insisting it would get her to my side faster. Jamie disagreed. No trip that involved waiting at the airport could beat him on the highway.

Mom agreed and settled into Jamie's BMW coupe. Dad and Lisa did the same, cramming their six-three frames into the bite-sized car. Jamie sped away. It was the only way he knew how to get around. When not finding rocket fuel leaks in Air Force aircraft, Jamie raced motorcycles professionally. He traveled across the country looking for the next race, reaching speeds over 190 miles per hour on his Suzuki. He won consistently. When he didn't come in first overall, he landed at the top of his age group.

Normally, my parents couldn't stomach Jamie's need for speed. They couldn't bear to watch their youngest son put his life on the line as he weaved his way along an asphalt track in the pursuit of prize money. I understood their fears. The first time I watched Jamie race in 1997 was—to put it mildly—terrible.

The race day started well, and Jamie impressed me with his ability to control that skittering piece of metal. When the final race queued up, I positioned myself on the back curves to watch. Soon after the race started, Jamie and two other racers took a turn side-by-side-by-side, with Jamie on the outside. The one in the middle lost control and slid into Jamie, knocking Jamie off his bike. The event was immediately black-flagged, putting an end to the race. I didn't know what happened at the time. I didn't see the accident. All I knew was Jamie wasn't coming around the track and the race was over. My heart convulsed.

Minutes felt like hours, but I eventually saw Jamie again. He had his helmet in his hand and was walking toward me. He was fine. The other racer, Jamie reported, was fine also. All was well. No one died—that time.

So, yes, Mom and Dad were right to worry about their boy. But that was on the motorcycle track. Inside the BMW with his knees pressed against the dashboard, Dad didn't flinch at the speedometer that never dropped below eighty-five. "I just want my son to be alive," he repeated to himself. "I just want my son to be alive."

With Dad's mantra as background music, the journey to Savannah became a time trial with heavy implications. Jamie shaved an hour off the six-hour trip, reaching the hospital in what could be record time. Upon arrival, the family was ushered into my broom closet-sized room—no more than two visitors at a time due to the room's size—to see my sad state with their own eyes. Thankful as I was to see them, I was under the spell of sedating medication and struggled to stay awake. My family didn't care that I kept falling asleep, but I did. I wanted to tell each of them how much I loved them, but I wasn't conscious long enough to get the words out.

Between medication-induced naps, another pain weighed more heavily. Would I ever see my grandson Jaden again? There was no answer, but with my body barely hanging on, I feared the worst.

Desperate to pull me from Death's door, Jamie begged my nurse for permission to stay with me. "I won't be any trouble," he asserted, "and I'll help with anything you need. I'll turn Mark over, fetch supplies—whatever you want." The nursing staff relented and allowed Jamie to stay by my side on a plastic chair. If I stretched my arms out to either side, I could touch the room's opposite walls, but there was room for Jamie. We'd spent a lifetime together—hunting and fishing, fighting, riding bikes. Now, in my hour of need, we were together again, Jamie refusing to leave my side.

That night was torture, yet another confirmation of Jamie's loyalty. Instead of sleeping in a comfy bed, hoping all would be well, my brother spent hour after hour caring for me, cleaning raisin-colored vomit out of my hair, and crying over my situation. I apologized without ceasing, sorry that he felt obliged to care for me, but Jamie didn't want to hear it. He wasn't bothered. He was thankful I was alive and was eager to keep me that way.

Hour after hour, nurses and technicians came in and out of my room, taking blood from my body or giving breathing treatments to fight my body's attempt to shut down. I grew weaker by the moment, atrophy progressing from one system to the next. My voice weakened, and I barely had enough breath to form a sentence. I wanted to die, to see Jesus face to face. I knew He loved me and that if I let go of this mangled body, I would be in His arms. No more pain. No more screaming.

Please, God. Make it end. Take my life.

He declined.

———

With the morning came new visitors. Jamie stepped out to make room for them.

Travis, my stepson and father of the grandchild I was forbidden from seeing, walked in with Gary Houston. The pairing surprised me. Gary was an engineer. He was also a deacon at Clingan Ridge Baptist, a pillar who had been at the church since its founding. We weren't particularly close, but Gary was always willing to serve in any capacity. Travis, on the other hand, hadn't been in church for some time. When he learned about my accident, that changed. Despite having no car, Travis somehow made it to the Sunday evening service. While there, he visited the restroom. One of his old friends joined him, and Travis explained my situation through tears.

"I just need to get down there," Travis cried.

A stall door creaked open and closed softly. Gary stepped out. "I'll take you down there," he said. "Let's go."

Gary drove through the night, but Travis was the one who looked exhausted. Concern pooled in his eyes as he scanned the room, eyed the tubes sticking out of me, and entered my world of machine beeps and blips.

I told Travis not to worry about me and to keep working at being a good father. Selfishly, I hoped my injury would open the door to seeing Jaden again. Perhaps Jaden's mom would feel so guilty over the accident that she would soften up and let me see my grandson. What's a little spine injury if I got to see Jaden?

"Bad things happen all the time," I said, resisting the urge to tug harder on Travis's heart strings. "No matter what happens, we need to stay together as a family." I encouraged Travis to repair his relationship with Jaden's mother. If my accident didn't give me access to Jaden, perhaps a renewed romance or civil friendship could.

Our conversation was short and inconclusive. Travis couldn't stomach much more. The IVs, pain, and uncertainty overwhelmed him and made him nauseous. I told him I understood and that I loved him.

Travis and Gary said their goodbyes and left.

Sometime later that day—Monday, September 21, 2009—nurses prepared me for surgery. Then they carted me to the operating room, where an anesthesiologist put me to sleep and settled down to monitor my vitals. As planned, Dr. Cannon's son-in-law sliced me open and yanked the guts out of my torso, clearing the way for surgery. For the next ten and one-half hours, Dr. Cannon used his experience and expertise to stabilize my spine.

Chapter 6

Introducing Billy Bob

THE SUN WARMED MY FACE as I awoke in a new room. A white sheet and blanket hid my legs and stomach, and my chest and abdomen were wrapped in a hard plastic cast—a turtle shell that hid whatever stitches lay beneath. Compared to the critical care bay where I spent the previous two nights in tears and terror, this room was huge. There was a couch, two chairs, and enough room for a dozen visitors. Beyond the foot of the bed was a giant bay window. The wall to my left had a second bay window. The blinds of both were wide open, giving the room a bright sheen.

I blinked away my blurry vision and looked up. A butterfly looked back at me. It was different from the one on the emergency department ceiling, but it could have been painted by the same person. Pinks, blues, greens, and thick outlines clung to the square tile overhead, posing the butterfly in a perpetual freeze-frame.

My room ebbed and flowed with people coming and going, their faces and voices no longer twisted in the drama of the previous days. Nurses informed me that the surgery went well. Dr. Cannon came in later and agreed.

As the day drew on, Dad and Lisa said their farewells. In addition to helping Mom with the counseling center, Dad oversaw two casket cases in the meat department at Walmart. Lisa was a case manager for Juvenile Judge Carrell Van Deacon, ensuring kids were at school and home at the right times. The responsibilities were pressing, and Dad and Lisa had to report to work the following day. Fortunately, Mom and Jamie stuck around. But even if they left, I wouldn't have been lonely.

The door to my room constantly swung open. Pastor Vaughn and a flood of friends poured in, their visits a blur of tears and prayers and statements echoing a single sentiment: "I'm so sorry this happened to you."

As each visitor entered my room, I flashed back to the last time we were together. One visitor at a time, I recalled our last interaction—where we were and what we were doing. Every memory featured an activity I suspected I would never do again.

For years, I was part of a church group that became known as the Pit Crew. Anytime the church needed to raise funds, the Pit Crew went into action, smoking Boston butts all night long for a barbecue fundraiser the following day. We knew our stuff, which was proven by the fact that we sold out every time.

Maybe I could hang out by a grill and make some barbecue. Maybe. But fishing and hunting, softball and other sports? They were out of the question.

I dozed as visitors tiptoed into my room, hugged me, and gave their well wishes, their voices made soft and distant by the medication. One visitor, however, yanked me out of my medication-induced stupor.

————————

I didn't expect Kelly Lewis to walk through my door. She worked at the church and helped me and others with various ministry needs. She was very sweet, but I didn't realize we were close enough for her to drive six hours to see me. It seemed odd, but not as odd as what Stacy did.

Soon as Kelly entered my room, Stacy picked up a handheld video camera and started recording. All my confusion cleared up when a second person entered.

Those who have met Billy Bob love him. The alter ego of Kelly Lewis's husband and fellow Pit Crew member Steve Lewis, Billy Bob appeared any time someone needed an object lesson on judging others. His origin story was in children's ministry. Wanting to teach children not to judge based on outward appearance, Steve put on a wig of long, stringy, oily hair and crammed a worn baseball cap on top of it. He wore a mouthful of fake gnarled teeth, ragged fingerless gloves, a dirty trench coat, and torn and tattered pants and shirt. He complemented the outfit with indecipherable guttural sounds and a hidden fart machine that got frequent use.

Billy Bob appeared at church multiple times over the

years. He also accompanied me on a trip to my parents' counseling center in Sweetwater, Tennessee. Dad was counseling a group of alcoholics in one room, while Mom counseled sex offenders in another. I brought pizza and introduced Billy Bob. Then, Billy Bob meandered off and sat by himself in the corner, looking pitiful without any pizza.

In the group of alcoholics, a lady made an offhand comment about Billy Bob's appearance. A gentleman in the same group had a different response. He motioned toward Billy Bob.

"I'm not eating until he eats."

The other reforming alcoholics agreed. The sex offenders had the same response. If Billy Bob didn't get any pizza, they didn't want any.

That day, I didn't teach a lesson. I learned one.

But I wasn't at church or a state-mandated therapy session for sex offenders or alcoholics. I was in a 622-bed hospital in Savannah, Georgia, and the caring professionals who staffed the hospital were suspicious of Billy Bob.

When Billy Bob dragged himself into my room, a cluster of nervous nurses trailed him, ready to pounce. Billy Bob ignored them. He pulled a chair to my bedside and plopped down. "Whatcha doin' layin' here, fur?"

The room erupted in laughter. Realizing Billy Bob wasn't a threat, the nurses relaxed and dispersed to care for other patients who weren't being visited by such striking guests.

I reached for Billy Bob's hand. When I touched it, Billy Bob's features softened. He pushed away a lock of shiny hair and transformed from Billy Bob the object lesson to Steve the friend.

I pushed down my bed covers and showed off my legs. They lay motionless below me, and I willed them to move. They obeyed in ridiculous slow motion.

Steve grabbed my arm. "Yeah, brother," he said, "you're going to walk out of here." His voice was somber and certain. I wanted to get up then and there to prove him right, but I was too weak. Yet, his words gave me faith to dream of walking again and filled me with confidence that even if I never took another step, everything would be okay. The King was still on the throne.

Steve and Kelly eventually left, and others took their place. Someone was by my side every hour of the day. Family refused to leave me on my own, afraid of what would happen in their absence. So, at least one of them stayed in my room at all times. When visiting hours ended, Jamie began his self-inflicted night shift. We did our best to sleep, but there were plenty of interruptions. This was a hospital, after all.

During those late nights, I often put Jamie to work. Stacy wasn't up to speed on our bills, so Jamie helped make sure they all got paid. I didn't know when I would get out of the hospital, but I didn't want to return home to a house with no electricity or water. I gave Jamie my log-in information, and he paid my bills online with his laptop.

Equally as important, I picked Jamie's brain to ensure my fantasy football team had the best chance at success. Each week, we ran through player options and who was likely to provide the most points based on the matchups.

At the time, I was a big Saints fan, and Drew Brees never spent much time on my fantasy bench.

Jamie also updated my CaringBridge website. He set up the site early on, and we often used our nights to write and edit updates. It was an easy way to keep friends and family in the loop without the hassle of texting, calling, or emailing everyone individually. It was a win-win. We posted updates, and with the click of a button, people could learn about the latest in my recovery and send messages of encouragement.

———————

"Mark, you need to eat something." Mom held a slice of pizza toward me.

Stacy echoed the sentiment. I'd not eaten for three days. But nothing sounded good, and I wasn't hungry. Besides, I didn't have the strength to eat. Just the thought of raising my arm wore me out.

Mom sat in her chair and repeated that I needed to eat. I lay back and looked up at the butterfly. "I know, Mom," I said quietly. "I just don't think I can."

Mom set her pizza down and pulled an apple out of her purse. She ran a knife in a continuous circle along the apple surface. In less than thirty seconds, she held a peeled Granny Smith apple in one hand. In the other, a long, skinny apple peel stretched out in a single thread.

She set the peel aside, cut the apple into slices, and tossed the core into the trash can. She offered me a slice, forcing me to choke down tears. Here I was, thirty-nine years old, being cared for by my mother like I were a child.

I grabbed the slice and bit into the apple slowly. Sparks flew! My first bite awakened every taste bud in my mouth. To this day, that remains the most delicious bite of apple I've ever taken.

Mom handed me one slice after another until I finished the whole thing. The process was excruciatingly slow, my every movement matching the speed of a three-toed sloth.

As the apple digested, a nurse came in and stabbed me with a needle. Apparently, the accident goofed up my body's insulin production, which meant I needed frequent insulin shots. Nurses also poked my finger to check my blood sugar levels. They poked so often that my fingertips went numb.

Improper insulin production was just the start of my issues. My kidneys were damaged, forcing me to urinate through a catheter. And lying in bed increased my risk for a number of health issues, including:

- **MRSA.** Hospitalization practically guarantees methicillin-resistant Staphylococcus aureus (MRSA). It's the highly contagious bacterial infection every hospitalized person dreads. Daily preventive antibiotics guarded against potential infection.

- **Pneumonia.** Since I was forced to lie on my back, there was a chance that pneumonia would settle into my lungs. I didn't want that. Neither did the hospital staff. They gave me an aspirator and told me to suck on it multiple times every day to fend off the disease.

• **Bed sores.** Sounds benign, but Christopher Reeves—the original Superman—died from bed sores. To keep me from the same fate, my brother and nurses turned me at least every hour, shifting me from one side to the other, then to my back.

Annoying as the breathing treatments, antibiotics, and insulin shots were, something bothered me more. My left foot was being stubborn. The day after surgery, it adopted an odd droop and refused to stay in place. Thanks to my biology background,* I knew some medical terminology. I informed a nurse that the gastrocnemius muscle in my left leg couldn't support the weight of my foot. She was as concerned with my foot as she was impressed with my use of medical jargon. At least I think she was impressed.

Regardless of how she esteemed my linguistic abilities, the nurse presented the issue to my doctor. He prescribed a boot to keep my foot in a fixed position, hoping the boot would correct the droop. *Spoiler alert: It didn't work.*

Around the time I got the boot, the medical staff began intruding on me more frequently. Instead of popping in every couple hours, they visited me every half hour, poking my belly and fingertips and checking my vitals. My family looked on with concern, as nurses and doctors whispered and evaluated me time and again.

---

* I taught anatomy and physiology at Bradley Central High School during a semester of student teaching. Then I taught at Cleveland High School in the place of a teacher who ran off to get filthy rich by selling his deceased father's coal mines. When the enriched teacher returned to town the next semester, he reclaimed his teaching position.

In the midst of the pricks and prods, I experienced a profound peace. I loved Jesus, and I longed for Him to bring me home and hold me in His arms. Once again, He had different plans.

Without warning, the pain returned. My body writhed. I didn't scream, but I was on the verge of letting loose. My medical team doped me up with more pain killers. Relief.

Meanwhile, Jamie dug around online. The folks at Memorial did a fine job, but Jamie felt I needed a higher level of care. He researched options that emphasized neurological care and found a rehabilitation facility he thought would better serve my needs. Located in Atlanta, Georgia, the Shepherd Center specializes in helping people recover from spinal cord and brain injuries. According to *U.S. News & World Report*, they're good at it—one of the best in America. Added benefit: It's only two hours from Cleveland. Being that close to home would make life easier on family and friends who wanted to visit.

Jamie pitched the idea of transferring, and I was sold instantly. The team at Memorial did their best, but Shepherd Center experts deal with spinal problems all day, every day. Their expertise could make a significant difference in my recovery.

The following day, a case manager came by. She understood my desire to go to Shepherd Center but was unsure it would work out. Memorial offered rehabilitation services and my transfer wasn't urgent, so there was no guarantee insurance would approve my request to go to Shepherd Center.

The case manager recommended we not get our hopes up. We didn't. We went to the source of our hope.

"Pray!" I told Jamie. "And have the church do the same."

Chapter 7

Bump, Bump, Ouch, Ouch

Early the next morning, the case manager knocked briefly on my door and walked in. "You've been approved," she said. "You'll transfer to Shepherd Center as soon as we can get you ready."

Thank you, Jesus!

A couple hours later, nine trauma physicians—one for each day I spent at Memorial—rounded to my room for a collective final look. I didn't recognize all of them, but I suspect most had something to do with my care.

"I know you probably never get told how amazing you are, so I'm telling you now," I said to the gathered group. "You saved my life, and the kindness you've shown me has been wonderful."

One doctor, a young female, held back tears with an affixed smile. I informed them all that I was a Christian. As a Christian, I considered them God's assistants. "You help people," I said. "You heal them, and that's a wonderful thing."

With the farewell meeting concluded, it was decision time. I'd already chosen to go to Shepherd Center. Now I had to pick my mode of transportation. Tempting as it was to take a helicopter—especially after being inches away from leaving the Nauti Dawg on one—the $13,000 price tag made me a little gun shy. Hitching a ride in an ambulance provided significant cost savings, clocking in at just three grand. But even that was a steep price, especially with the medical bills already piling up (not to mention the destroyed swim trunks I had to replace). Seeing my dilemma, Mom offered to pay for my ride. She insisted I could pay her back later when we were all safe and sound in Cleveland. So, I swallowed my pride and borrowed cash from Mom for the third and cheapest option: medical transport.

A couple days later, a nurse carted me out of my room, transferred me to another gurney, and lifted me into the back of a retired ambulance. The outside of the automobile was repainted with the transport company's logo. Inside looked like a typical ambulance, but because it wasn't part of any hospital system, the one-way trip to Atlanta only cost $1,300.

To my left sat a female EMT wearing a ponytail and a maroon shirt with the transport company's logo. Up front, a second EMT in a matching company-approved shirt handled the driving. Before we took off, Jamie spoke with the transport team and learned they didn't know where Shepherd Center was. That was music to Jamie's ears. He used the opening to take control of the situation.

"No problem," he said. "Follow me."

Not knowing Jamie's history of motorcycle racing, the transport team agreed to the plan. Since Jamie had already researched the fastest route to the Center, he would lead the pack in his BMW. The EMTs would follow with me in tow, and Mom and Stacy would bring up the rear in my red Ford Explorer.

Before taking off, we agreed on some simple hand signals so I could communicate with Mom and Stacy on the trip. Three fingers meant all was well and doubled as "I love you." Four, "I love you, too." I'm not sure why we didn't just chat on our cell phones, but we felt pretty clever with our low-tech communication system.

The first hour went without incident. I was at ease as I told the ride-along EMT about my accident and apprehensions of the future. Between stories, I dozed off and on, courtesy of whatever pain medication coursed through my veins. Every time I woke up, the nurse patted my arm or leg and made sure I was okay. Then I looked out the back window and raised three fingers to Stacy and Mom.

With Jamie serving as the pace car for our journey, the trip moved along quickly. I don't know how fast we drove, but we made good time.

Two hours into the trip, I woke up. All was well in the transport mobile. Mom and Stacy were in sight, so I raised three fingers. They sent back smiles and four fingers. I made small talk with the female EMT.

Another hour passed, and our repurposed ambulance entered a construction zone. The once-smooth road became a thing of the past. Cracks and potholes grabbed and punched at our tires. The interior of the transport vehicle rattled and hummed. One after another, the bumps shook the vehicle and everything in it—including me.

"Can we change lanes?" I asked. Something was wrong. I felt dizzy and weak. The pain pills had worn off, and the pain started again. My body was clammy with sweat.

The female EMT placed a wet washcloth on my forehead, then draped it across my wrist to cool me down. It was then that I discovered a fatal flaw in our hand-based communication plan. I only knew how to sign one thing: *I love you and things are great in here.* Now, I was too weak to hold up three fingers, and I didn't know how to tell Mom and Stacy the tides had turned.

"Keep your eyes open." The EMT held my hand and spoke with a firm gentleness mastered by generations of Southern women. "Don't go to sleep, Mark. Stay awake."

I didn't want to go to sleep, but I didn't have a choice. And if I didn't get to the Shepherd Center soon, my final rest would begin inside a $1,300-per-ride repurposed ambulance.

The final hour was a moment-by-moment struggle against a growing weakness that threatened to pull me under. Regret plagued me. I should have taken the helicopter! I decided if I ever got the opportunity again, I would hop in the chopper, no questions asked.*

Somehow, I survived another ride I expected to be my last. The transport team unloaded me around three-thirty that afternoon and helped me transition to a Shepherd Center gurney.

"He's a little weak," the female EMT said. "The trip may have taken something out of him."

A little weak? Something out of him? I'm knocking on Death's door!

The receiving team nodded. They were used to weak, sick people who felt worse after transport, so they weren't concerned. But this was more than travel-induced weakness. I felt I'd taken three steps backward in my recovery. My feelings must have shown. Stacy, Mom, and Jamie noticed a difference and mentioned it to my care team. However, the medical experts insisted it was normal to feel worse after a long ride. Their confidence put my family at ease.

Assured I was fine, Mom, Jamie, and Stacy left to find accommodations for the coming days. Helpless, I lay on my back as Shepherd Center staff pushed me down the hallway. Rolling past the check-in desk, I again found my attention affixed on the ceiling. Amid countless white tiles, a hand-painted butterfly floated on a single tile. Its

_____

*A decade later, I finally rode in a helicopter after a head-on collision. The accident happened out in the country, down the street from my home. I called 911, explained I had a previous spinal cord injury, and stated that I suspected I broke my back again. Soon, a Life Force helicopter descended on the scene and whisked me away to Erlanger Hospital in Chattanooga, Tennessee. Thankfully, I did not break my back a second time.

yellows, pinks, greens, and blues disappeared as a nurse pushed me onward on my wheeled bed.

Inside a small room, curtains hung from the ceiling and dangled three feet from the floor, sectioning the space into four bite-sized compartments with minimum privacy. I didn't need privacy though. That need went out the window when a nurse cut my swimsuit off. What I needed was good care.

————————

Before leaving Memorial, the staff disconnected all IV access and pulled all the sticky leads off my chest. I entered Shepherd Center with bare arms and chest, no IV fluids or pain medication dripping into my veins, no wires hanging from my chest to help staff monitor my vitals.

The nurse wheeled my gurney into position and left.

My heart skipped a beat. Maybe it was a mistake to come to Shepherd Center. Maybe I transferred here to die. Maybe God knew I wasn't going to live long, and He wanted me closer to home when I took my final breath. I lay with these fears tumbling inside my brain for nearly three hours. My only distraction came courtesy of one of my three roommates.

His bed was to my left, and he must have loved economics. Every waking moment, he listened to a cassette tape about economics over and over. I'm not sure if he was memorizing the content or using it as a sedative, but it drove me to the brink of insanity. Fortunately, he turned it off when his girlfriend came to visit. Unfortunately, their conversation filtered through the fabric divider and was cut short when his girlfriend announced she was calling it quits on their relationship.

"I don't think I'm going to be able to handle this," she said before seeing herself to the door.

The tape started up again and played all night. As the taped voice repeated itself, I couldn't help but have two thoughts:

1. I would have dumped that guy, too. From what I could tell, he was as dull as a used crayon. His hospitalization probably answered the question his now ex-girlfriend asked herself for months: *How do I get out of this relationship?*

2. Would Stacy, my wife of nearly a dozen years, dump me? Would this be too much for her to handle? Over the next few months, I would repeatedly acknowledge that recovery was going to be hard on both of us. I told her over and over that I would understand if she wanted to leave, to find an easier life. Stacy insisted she didn't, even after I told her about my sad-sack roomie getting the boot.

The night nurse appeared after seven that evening. He was a kind man. He was also muscular, which meant he would have no trouble rolling me from side to side to prevent bed sores. Sweet as my nurses at Memorial were, I cringed when it was time to change positions. They jerked and tugged on the sheet multiple times to put me in a new position, and their movements were harsh and painful. I imagined my buff new nurse had the strength to turn me in a single, fluid motion that didn't leave me in pain.

Encouraged to be in his care, I mentioned that something felt off, and I needed someone to look me over. The nurse grinned a grin of someone who hears that every hour of every shift. "You'll be fine," he insisted.

I took his word as truth. His pecs were too large to argue with.

The hours passed, each one taking another bit of my strength. It was nearly midnight when I pressed the call button for my nurse. "Something's wrong with me," I repeated when he walked into my curtained room.

"Hey buddy, I get it. You're in a new place, and everything feels a little off." He crossed his arms, which caused his biceps to swell. "Trust me—you couldn't be in a better place than you're in now."

Translation: Of course something was wrong with me. Otherwise, I wouldn't be filling a bed at Shepherd Center. But I wasn't in bad enough shape to demand immediate attention.

"Can I get a Gatorade?" I asked. Gatorade was never my go-to drink, but it sounded good at the moment.

Nurse Muscles brought a cup of ice and filled it with lemon-lime Gatorade. I started sipping around eight o'clock and never stopped. I had a hard time sleeping, and without Jamie there to talk to, there was nothing else to do but drink. So, I downed bottle after bottle. It tasted great, like it was meeting some deep need. I learned later that it was. My body was drained of electrolytes, and Gatorade helped me replenish. As long as I kept drinking, I fended off the strange feelings of sickness that started on the ride to Shepherd Center.

The following morning, my trash can overflowed with empty Gatorade containers. I was ten days post-accident and ten days separated from the last time I washed my body. A small, quiet nurse tech announced she was going to give me a shower. I was in no position to argue. I needed a good cleaning, and I couldn't do it on my own.

She positioned a sling behind my back, connected the sling to a Hoyer lift with a series of hooks, and started working a pump. Slowly, my body rose from the bed— first my back and legs, then my rump. Hovering above my bed in the sling, I lost my bearings and felt out of control. The room spun around me as the tech moved me to the shower area. Once she set me in the shower chair, the spinning slowed.

She cleaned every area of my body not hidden under the turtle shell. What would have been scandalously unforgettable a week earlier—having a strange woman bathe me—turned out to be a remarkably bland experience. My only memory was how good it felt to be clean.

Shower finished, the tech dried me off, then lifted me with the Hoyer. The room rotated underneath me. I hung limp and dizzy as the tech balled up the dirty bed sheets and grabbed a plastic bag. With one fluid motion, she swung the bag from her head to her waist, forcing air into the bag with a tremendous sound. The noise sent the room into turbo spin and intensified my senses—every sound became horrifically loud, every light excessively bright.

Unfazed, the nurse tech tossed the dirty sheets in the bag and set the bag on the ground. But I was still in Dizzytown, the sound of the opening bag still ringing in my ears. The nurse eased me into bed, covered my naked lower half with a sheet, glanced at me, and left.

Moments later, a female doctor marched with purpose to my bedside. "Mr. Wells," she said without introduction, "stick out your tongue."

She didn't seem interested in hearing about my dizziness or sensory overload, so I followed her direction. She frowned.

"Mr. Wells, your tongue is white," she continued. "You're bleeding internally."

Chapter 8

World Turned Upside Down

THE ROOM TWISTED AND TURNED, and my head went along for the ride.

"In the next few moments," this unnamed doctor said, "I'll need you to sign some papers for me."

Papers? I thought. *I'm bleeding internally and can't see straight, but they won't do anything about it until I sign some papers?* None of those thoughts escaped my lips. All I said was, "What papers?"

The doctor produced a thin stack of medical forms and pointed at the document on top. "This one's so I can give you blood."

I signed immediately and asked if she was going to put me to sleep.

She shook her head. "No time for that. I need to save your life." She handed me another paper—this one granting permission to do the procedure without anesthesia.

I signed it, then I signed a few others. I didn't care what any of them said. There was no time. The doctor made that clear.

"Now," she said, "this next part is gonna hurt."

"Wait," I said. "Aren't you going to give me something to numb the pain?"

Additional medical staff flooded into the room. Even with the room full of people, I felt scared and alone. Afterward, I learned I wasn't completely alone. My family wasn't in the room with me, but they were nearby. The doctor labeled me a code blue—shorthand for "This guy's going to die if we don't do something"—and commanded that someone call my family back to the hospital. Mom, Jamie, and Stacy arrived at the waiting room just in time to see a nurse rush a crash cart—the cart used when "This guy's going to die if we don't do something"—to my room.

The doctor gave me a motherly look. "No," she said. "Nothing to numb the pain. We don't have time for that either."

I permitted the doctor to do whatever she had to do and again wondered if this was where I would die, at a renowned neurologic rehabilitation hospital under the hand of an unnamed doctor after getting my first shower in a week and a half.

The doctor removed my turtle shell. "I'm putting a PICC line in," she announced. For non-medical folks, PICC is short for *peripherally inserted central catheter*. It's how doctors and nurses give intravenous medication and—in my case at that moment—blood. She placed the line below my collar bone in the subclavian vein, then turned her attention to my shoulder.

Her team covered me in surgical drapes, leaving a small opening over my left collar bone. Mercifully, one of the drapes covered my face. I wouldn't have to see what was about to take place. And despite her initial plan, the doctor gave me a quick shot of anesthetic near the surgical site to take the edge off.

The cold scalpel slid across my collar bone. I winced and grimaced as forceps pulled at my skin. The doctor wiped a bloodied instrument on the surgical drape covering my face.

Though I took pride in my ability to understand medical terminology, I was grossly outmatched by the situation. Every other word introduced new-to-me medical jargon. The long words came from every corner of my curtain-walled room. Then, I heard a sentence that made sense—though I wasn't sure it was true.

"Mark," someone said from behind the surgical drape covering my face, "you're doing great."

"I'm scared." I was weak and tired.

More medical jargon, more tugging on the skin over my collar bone, and then the doctor spoke in plain English. "Mr. Wells, I'm going to stick a chest tube into your left side."

The doctor placed a hand on my side for leverage and leaned toward me. Before I could think of any questions to ask, a gunshot echoed through the room. There was no screaming, and no one hit the floor to dodge the bullet.

Relief washed over me. All those close calls caught up to me. I was finally dead.

"Mr. Wells?" The doctor removed the drape covering my face.

I opened my eyes, surprised to still be in a hospital room surrounded by medical personnel. Surprised to be alive. "Yes?"

"You're going to be okay." The doctor gave her staff some brief orders, tossed her bloodied, once-sterile gloves in the biohazard disposal on the wall, and exited.

The nurses began cleaning the area around my new incision. While they wiped me down and disposed of surgical drapes, blood flowed through the chest tube into a dispenser behind me. The nurses connected me to a blood transfusion machine and explained what went down.

Apparently, I'd been bleeding internally for a while. Nearly half of my body's blood had seeped into my pleural cavity, the area between the lungs and chest cavity. It all started during my medical transport ride to Atlanta, when the rough ride shook some surgical stitches loose. The buildup caused me to feel dizzy and weak. Twenty more minutes, and I could have been dead.

But God again had different plans. The nurse tech who bathed me noticed something—the crazy look in my eyes, perhaps the pile of Gatorade empties in the trash—and sprinted to fetch the on-call doctor. Then the doc jammed a tube into my chest, giving the misplaced blood an escape route out of my body. That was the sound I mistook for a gunshot: the tube breaking into my pleural cavity, a gross, generous gift from above.

Recently showered and more recently cleaned up after emergency surgery inside my four-person curtained room, I breathed deeply as the team moved me to the intensive care unit (ICU) for post-surgery recovery.

————————

As part of my treatment plan, the ICU literally turned my world upside down. There was still blood in my pleural cavity, so the ICU nurses tipped me in different directions to get it out. Every half hour, a nurse tilted my bed fifteen degrees, lifting either my head or my feet as high as the hospital bed could go. This is called the Trendelenburg position. It felt more like Terribleburg, as I constantly felt at risk for sliding out of bed and onto the floor. I endured this topsy-turvy, heads-up, heads-down ordeal for two days straight, as the misplaced blood dribbled slowly out of my body.

While draining, I was in the glass-doored room nearest the nurse's station. Stacy said that's where patients go who need the most diligent monitoring. It was also the room with the best view of the world beyond the ICU. From my tilted perch, I watched people come and go, a parade of hurting people seeking hope and healing. My odd angle distorted the world a bit, but the pain I saw was crystal clear.

That pain reached a crescendo during my final day in the ICU. I was resting as comfortably as I could with my head at a fifteen-degree angle when a cluster of medical staff stampeded past. Another ICU patient was in the midst of a code blue. Medical personnel shouted orders and vital readings at one another for ten minutes, and then the commotion dwindled. One by one, staff members quietly filed out of the ICU, grieving their failed efforts and the death of a patient.

My remaining hours in the ICU were marked by frequent checkups and more bed tilting. Eventually, I was told the tilting did its job. Almost all of the blood was out of my pleural cavity, and it was time to move to a new room.

———————

It wasn't private, but my new room was worlds better than the curtained closet I shared with three others. Or it would be better once they got clean sheets on the bed.

I lay on a gurney as a nurse stripped the used sheets and stuffed them in a trash bag. A large butterfly was imprinted on the bare mattress. I rested my head on my gurney as the nurse wrapped butterfly-patterned sheets around the mattress corners. I looked up. A butterfly clung to the ceiling tile overhead, painted in place with thick black outlines and bright pastels. The nurse alerted me that everything was ready, then transferred me to the freshly sheeted hospital bed. I thanked her. As she strode away, I noticed her scrubs and hair clasp. Both featured butterflies.

Across the room, a middle-aged man sat in a chair

and watched the whole event. I settled into my new space, and the gentleman introduced himself as James. He explained that his brother, Wayne, crashed his S10 Chevy while driving drunk. Wayne escaped without injury, but James's seventeen-year-old son, Eric—who was asleep in the passenger seat—woke up in the hospital, paralyzed from the neck down.

I'd spent the previous two weeks pitying my plight, asking why God allowed me to suffer, and I'd not come up with any reasons. Now I was splitting a room with a kid half my age who had his whole life before him and would be spending it in a wheelchair.

Heartbroken and convicted, I didn't know how to respond, how to encourage Eric. So, I stayed quiet. It was evening, and I was exhausted. Thankfully, Eric wasn't offended. Neither of us were going anywhere anytime soon. We could catch up and compare scars later.

The next day, Eric and I chatted about our accidents and previous lives. Eric was an outgoing high schooler who loved baseball and the Georgia Bulldogs. Despite his love for UGA (VFL*), I liked Eric immediately. I got along well with his parents also, which was good, since they were always in the room.

Post-accident, Eric was fitted with a tracheostomy. The plastic tube rested in a hole in his throat and helped him breathe—most of the time. At other times, Eric choked on it. A nurse often came in to clean the tube out. Eric

---

*For the uneducated, VFL is short for "Vol for Life." It indicates loyalty to the beloved Volunteers from the University of Tennessee at Knoxville.

apologized every time, as if he purposefully clogged the device or had anything to do with his present state. And in his darker moments, he admitted to suicidal thoughts, unsure if he could move forward with a life featuring below-the-neck paralysis and tracheostomy.

I grieved with Eric and did what I could to improve his mood, telling jokes and singing "The Crawdad Song."

You get a line and I'll get a pole, honey.
You get a line and I'll get a pole, babe.
You get a line and I'll get a pole.
We'll go down to the crawdad hole—
Honey, baby, mine.

While Eric and I got off to a good start, a growing tension within my family reached its crescendo. Stacy didn't want my brother, Jamie, staying in the hospital room with me.

The problem started days earlier at Memorial. Immediately after my back surgery, a nurse stepped into the waiting room to give an update on my status. She called for Mrs. Wells. Since Stacy was in the bathroom at the time, Mom took her place. She was, after all, Mrs. Wells, and she wanted to learn my status so she could update Stacy and the rest of the family.

When Stacy came out of the restroom, she was furious. "Your mom should have asked the nurse to wait," she told me later. "She had no right to receive news about your procedure when I wasn't there." This was followed up with a heart-wrenching ultimatum. "It's me or them," she said. "You've got to choose between your wife and the rest of your family. What's it going to be?"

Every moment afterward bubbled with tension—a kind of stress I'd never experienced before. Stacy always got along with my family. This sudden change caught me off guard.

Despite the oddity of it all, the choice was obvious. I had to pick my wife without throwing her under the bus in the process. Somehow, I needed to choose Stacy and reject the rest of my family without letting anyone know it was Stacy's idea.

This was complicated by my generous brother, Jamie, who stayed with me every night at Memorial. Night after night, Stacy's command that I make my decision ate at me. I was careful not to spill the beans, but Jamie knew something wasn't quite right. When he asked, I insisted it was just the accident. The balancing act was mentally and emotionally draining. I needed my family members— every one of them. But Stacy wouldn't allow it.

At the Shepherd Center, Jamie expected to take his post and stay with me overnight. Stacy wasn't going to let that happen. "Make your choice," she said. "But if Jamie doesn't leave, I'm calling security."

Backed into a corner, I chose Stacy. Making the decision was the easy part. Breaking the news to Jamie was the hard part. Anger flared and burned hotter than my damaged legs ever did. Jamie, Stacy, Mom, Dad, and Lisa fumed.

While they stormed away, I was left crying in my

room behind a curtain that served as a bedroom wall, hurting not from my boat accident but the mess that was my family.

Eric's dad, James, overheard me.

"This is tough," James admitted. "We're going through a lot of the same situations, but if you ever need anything at all, don't hesitate to ask. I'm here for you."

It was a sweet sentiment, but I wished James wasn't there. Not that I didn't appreciate him during regular business hours. He was a great companion and father to Eric when the sun was shining. But at night, James turned into a freight train, and his nonstop snoring kept me from good sleep.

Some nights, Eric and I yelled at James to wake up. If James stirred and stopped snoring for a moment, the race was on, as Eric and I attempted to fall asleep before James dozed off again. Usually, Eric succeeded, leaving me awake on my own, staring at a painted butterfly, dreaming of a good night's sleep.

Chapter 9

Progress & Humility

ON MY FIRST DAY ROOMING with Eric, I met my main physician, Dr. Anna Elmers. She came by for a consultation, bringing a can-do attitude, a brilliant smile, and a series of X-rays that showed my injury and my newly installed stabilization cage. She wouldn't tell me exactly what to expect moving forward, but she insisted I could lead a normal life—with some challenges.

I hurled questions at her. *Would I regain sexual function? How about bladder and bowel control? How long will rehab take?*

Dr. Elmers encouraged me to be patient and promised I would get answers. Most answers, she said, would come through the Center's patient education program. Before I could get into those classes, however, I needed a second surgery. There was still some bad blood floating around inside my pleural cavity. A surgeon needed to hose everything down to clean it all out.

I called my parents to fill them in, and they gave the worst possible reply: "We're coming."

Stacy shook her head. My parents were not welcome. "Don't come," I said. "It's not a major operation."

Mom and Dad didn't want to hear it. "You almost died," Mom replied. "We're coming."

"I did almost die," I said quickly, "but we're past that. They'll clean me up, and everything will be fine. I'll call you afterward to tell you how it went."

Mom and Dad huffed on the other end of the phone line but agreed to stay home. Fortunately, surgery went as expected. The surgeon poked a few small holes in my side, hosed out my insides, and closed me up.

While my parents nursed their emotional pain, I started to recover physically. The most notable change was my voice. It got stronger, and I didn't whisper as much.

Soon, my days of lying in bed ended. For the next two-and-a-half months, nearly every waking moment was programmed and claimed by a therapist or educator.

Mornings started with an hour of counseling. I talked about fears and frustrations, how the tension in my family affected me and what I wanted out of life moving forward. There was a lot to process after a spinal cord injury, and I did my best to work through it all. On days when I opened up, I learned a lot.

After counseling, I wheeled over to an hour-long, mixed-sex class that answered some of my most pressing questions. For those interested, marital intimacy would likely be possible. However, I was told I should expect more trouble in that realm than women in the same boat.*

The remainder of each day was occupied by my occupational and physical therapists.

———————

As an occupational therapist, Emily was tasked with helping me function independently. She did this by teaching me to perform tasks of daily living.

Initially, it was hard to get dressed. I struggled to pull on my shoes and socks, and I didn't have the strength and flexibility necessary to bathe myself. Progress was slow but steady. Thanks to Emily's meticulous attention to detail and my dedication, I could soon dress myself.

A few weeks into therapy, Emily accompanied me out of the hospital and down the street to a nearby market. It wasn't a date. It was part of therapy. I was a married man, after all.

The trip to the store was easy—downhill all the way. I maneuvered my wheelchair around large cracks in the sidewalk and kept the chair from picking up excessive speed with little effort.

The way back was a chore. All the downhill sections were now uphill sections, and it took everything in me to climb my way back to the Center. Once I did, I headed to the rehab kitchen, where staff helped rehabbers relearn kitchen skills. There, I used the ingredients I purchased to

———————

Sorry for the boat pun.

make chicken, rice, and vegetable soup. Like my jokes, the soup was a hit. Staff members and my classmates asked for second and even third helpings.

A few days later, Dr. Elmers removed my turtle shell permanently. I'd healed up nicely, and rehab would advance quicker without the stiff, protective mechanism.

Losing the shell brought mixed emotions. When I wore the shell, it was impossible to bend over. It also stunk to high heaven. So, I was thrilled to regain some upper body mobility and get out of that stinking thing. But I was nervous. While the turtle shell looked ridiculous and reeked from six weeks of sweat, it kept me safe. I explained this to Dr. Elmers, and she repeated: "The shell goes."

Without the burden of my turtle shell, therapy entered new territory—the shower. Emily picked me up from my room and escorted me to the shower room outside of the Center's Olympic-sized pool. Then she walked me through the process of transferring from my wheelchair to a shower chair. She wanted to make sure I could do the transfer on my own without falling.

In just a few minutes, I mastered the technique. Not to brag, but it was fairly simple, even with my dad bod. I sat smugly in the plastic shower chair, wearing a new swimsuit and awaiting Emily's permission to climb back into my wheelchair. Her permission never came. Instead, she gave a command: "Now, turn the water on." An odd request, but I followed her directions. Water shot at me through the showerhead.

"What are you doing?" Emily asked.

I tilted my head in response, water bouncing off my

chest. I did everything Emily requested. I was sitting on a shower chair with water spraying at me, all at her direction. What more did she want?

"Lose the trunks."

My long-lost modesty returned with renewed vigor, heating my face and stealing my cognitive abilities. "What?" I stammered, hoping I'd heard her wrong. "But—why?"

Emily shrugged. "Before you leave, I need to make sure you know how to do everything." She pretended to scrub her back with an imaginary wash cloth. "That includes cleaning yourself—front, back, all the places."

"But . . . but, I see you every day," I said. "We work together. That's kind of . . ."

Emily dismissed my comment. "If it makes you feel any better, we have to do this again next week. When we do," she said, "your wife will be in here."

It didn't make me feel any better. If anything, the thought of showering in front of two women—my wife and my occupational therapist—was exceedingly awkward. Emily disagreed. For her, it was business as usual.

I put up a fight to no avail. Emily insisted her years as a therapist dulled the effects of the male physique on her mental health, so I eventually obeyed her absurd order to "Lose the trunks."

My entire body flush with embarrassment, I washed myself for the first time in two months. More showers followed, each monitored by my wife or a paid medical professional. The embarrassment dulled but never quite disappeared.

I also learned to transfer from the bed to my wheelchair and vice versa, another activity that required monitoring.

Frustrating as it was to be under constant surveillance, it was necessary. I even grew to appreciate watchful eyes thanks to a misadventure with my roommate, Eric, and a northern rehabber named Jared.

———————

Shepherd Center is home to a wheelchair rugby team. When Eric, Jared, and I learned of an upcoming practice, we decided to check it out. We wheeled ourselves to the gym and looked on as the players crashed their wheelchairs, flung the ball to teammates, and raced down the court to score. It was chaotic, impressive, high-octane athleticism.

As we watched, Jared did what we were all told to do. It didn't matter if we were in physical therapy or at lunch, we were told to keep moving. Staying in motion increased our odds of improved mobility and function.

A common movement wheelchair-bound rehabbers perform is a weight transfer. Basically, you move forward, backward, or side to side to take pressure off whatever part of your rear end you're currently sitting on. It's another way to avoid pressure sores while increasing upper body and core strength.

Jared had done a million weight transfers, but none ended quite like this one. While the rugby team rammed into one another on the court, Jared leaned a little to the right, then a little more. The extra lean was too much for his weak core, and he fell over the side of his chair with a grunt.

When Eric and I noticed Jared's dilemma, we did what we did best: laugh. Jared laughed too, unsure how he would return to an upright position.

Fortunately, our horse laughter got the attention of the able-bodied rugby coach. He walked our way, found out what was going on, and hoisted Jared into a sitting position. After wiping away tears of laughter, Jared, Eric, and I made a pact. Our group would never again go on a trip without the accompaniment of at least one able-bodied person.

Perhaps, I hoped, I would be one of those able-bodied people in the future.

My mother held onto the same hope. She wanted to see her boy back on his feet, literally and figuratively. That's why she bought me five new pairs of Adidas exercise pants in various colors and a pair of squeaky-clean tennis shoes, making me the best-dressed rehabber at the whole facility.

And the new duds worked their magic. I was making progress. My upper body strength was returning.

Early on, I couldn't lift a one-pound weight in occupational therapy. A month into rehab, I was flinging eight pounders around like they were—well, eight-pound weights. My lower body was growing stronger as well. Inspired by my progress, Dr. Elmers and my physical therapist suggested I give walking a go.

———

Everything started out as planned. I looked sharp in my black Adidas pants and black, white, and grey Nike shoes. Jenn, my physical therapist, stood in front of me and encouraged me to get to my feet. A therapy tech stood behind me, holding my wheelchair in place in case my legs gave out and I needed an emergency rescue.

The Shower Incident of 2009 hadn't happened yet, so I still donned my turtle shell and dignity. I grabbed the parallel bars and pushed up. Jenn pulled at my turtle shell to help me out of my wheelchair. Then, I was on my feet.

For the first time in weeks, I stood up. My legs shook from the effort, and my heart raced with pride and possibility. Then, something tumbled out of the bottom of my Adidas pants and rolled to a stop between my Nikes.

Chapter 10

The Long Walk Home

Poop. I pooped my pants. And the poop rolled out of my pants.

"Don't worry about it," Jenn said, her effortless beauty rivaling that of a *Price Is Right* model. "It happens all the time. It's normal."

I stared at the small pile by my feet. "No," I said, "it's not normal."

But it was common—very common. Many patients at Shepherd Center had nonfunctional sphincter muscles, and I was one of them. With a dysfunctional sphincter, there's no way to stop the effects of gravity. If something is positioned at the right place (or wrong place, depending on your perspective), it's going to come out when given a chance. I learned that when I got to my feet for the first time in my fancy new clothes and shoes.

After a quick cleanup, I got back to work. Jenn helped me stand up and sit down over and over. The effort taxed my arms and legs. My body begged for rest, to stop pushing so hard, but I wasn't giving up—not with the opportunity to walk in front of me.

Jenn rested her hands on my torso, ready to act if my legs gave way. Then she took a small step backward, away from me. I gripped the parallel bars and swung my left foot forward. It landed. Jenn moved to give room for my right foot. I swung it into place, just ahead and to the right of my left foot. I repeated the motions, one foot after the other. Slowly, I made my way down the walking path, holding my weight with my arms and readjusting when I got too zealous and flung one foot directly in front of the other. I moved like a drunk person, but I was doing it. I was walking.[*]

After thirteen steps—seven with my left foot and six with my right, I reached the end of the barred path. Jenn helped me ease back into my chair. And like that, my first post-accident walk came to a conclusion. The whole event took just ninety seconds, but it felt like an eternity. Steve (a.k.a. Billy Bob) was right. I was going to walk again.

More encouragement came during recreational therapy. The therapist, Nick, learned that I enjoyed hunting and fishing. "You can still do that," he said.

I was surprised and excited. I told my brother and brother-in-law, and both agreed to take me out on the water and into the woods once I returned home. Maybe life wasn't over. Maybe I could still have a little fun.

Nick set up an air-rifle shooting range in the gym to

Visit tinyurl.com/4u8vrjdz for video evidence of my first steps.

let me show off my skill. I don't know if I hit the bulls-eye or left dents in the gym wall. All I remember was a surge of hope.

Communicating this hope, however, required tact. I wanted to shout from the rooftops and tell the world about my progress. But I couldn't, not in good conscience. My roommate, Eric, was a seventeen-year-old quadriplegic. He wasn't improving, and he wasn't expected to ever walk again. He was happy for me when he learned of my progress, but it felt wrong to dwell on my successes. So, I didn't.

That said, those first few steps lit a fire within me. I had a new goal. I was going to walk again, without bars for balance. Driven by that vision, I pushed myself every day. I pushed so hard that I transferred to outpatient therapy while I was still an inpatient.

In outpatient therapy, I focused entirely on relearning to walk. The therapist put me in a harness that supported my weight while I stood on a treadmill. After a month of no use, my legs were severely atrophied. A special machine moved my legs for me, retraining my brain and muscles to move and walk. Developing new muscle memory was painful, and I struggled to keep up with the machine's demands. But I carried on. My therapists made sure of it.

By the time I was discharged from Shepherd Center, I could walk a few steps with a walker and constant monitoring and pain. I was still wobbly on my feet and needed assistance. Though I suspected I would need a walker the rest of my life, I didn't have much to complain about. I was mobile, I was alive, and I was going home.

Stacy coasted through the parking lot, disappearing my nurse from the rearview mirror.

"You okay?" Stacy turned on the blinker and eased onto Peachtree Road.

I looked out my side window, which was suddenly blurry. "They're so nice," I said. "I hate leaving them. They're wonderful people."

It was true. I did hate leaving Shepherd Center. Everyone there—doctors, nurses, janitors, cooks, therapists, patients—were wonderful. They were also my safety net. With them nearby, I didn't fear falling. I didn't have to determine what step to take for continued recovery. They made sure I never fell and told me what to do every hour of every day. Recovery and companionship were guaranteed under their roof.

Sitting in the passenger seat on December 19, 2009, all that was gone. I wouldn't be surrounded by people who know what it's like to be paralyzed. No one would remind me to exercise every fifteen minutes. There would be no more opportunities to prank medical staff by placing melted chocolate bars under my leg. "Mama"—that's what I called my nurse tech—"I had an accident." I was on my own. If I was going to get out of that wheelchair for good, I would have to find a way. No one would do it for me.

At least that's how I felt. The reality was quite different. I was going home with my wife of a dozen years, who was prepared to care for my every need. My parents and siblings were willing to look beyond the hurt Stacy caused and were eager to lend a hand anywhere it was needed. Countless people at church prayed for me and looked forward to serving me face to face. And I was continuing therapy.

To top it off, another relational healing took place.

It had been months since Travis called it quits with Jaden's mother and moved back home. After getting discharged, I saw Travis every day and benefited from Travis's parental rights. For the first time in half a year, I got to hold my grandson—a bona fide Christmas miracle.

Praise God from whom all blessings flow!

––––––––––

Physical therapy started in January. Three days a week, I trekked forty-five minutes to downtown Chattanooga for three-hour sessions at Siskin Hospital for Rehabilitation. Jeff Davis drove me. We met at Cleveland Utilities years earlier and remained friends after his retirement. Jeff watched me take my first steps at the Shepherd Center, and he was excited to play a role in my ongoing recovery.

The first hour of therapy was led by a fellow in a wheelchair. We did all sorts of bizarre movements, many that wouldn't have felt like exercise if I wasn't recovering from a spinal cord injury. Sometimes, I just sat on an exercise ball for as long as I could. Other times, I jumped in a pool and floated around.

The second and third hours were closer to typical physical therapy. My therapist helped me stretch for a while, then we ran through an assortment of exercises to work specific muscles affected by the accident. Nearly every session, I walked with assistance.

When rehab wasn't on the schedule, I hit the gym, thanks to Todd Sparks. Todd was a friend who played on my church softball team. When he learned I wanted to push myself outside of rehab, he volunteered to drive me to the Cleveland YMCA. I accepted his offer.

At the Y, I worked my upper and lower body every way possible. I lifted free weights, sweated away on elliptical machines, and yanked on half a dozen pulley machines. I was committed to squeezing every bit of use from my damaged body, and it paid off.

I gained strength and mobility. After two weeks, I graduated from my wheelchair to a cane. Then I dropped to two days a week at Siskin and started going to the Y three days. The gains kept coming. That's when Jeff decided to test my strength and coordination in an unconventional manner.

On the way home from a Siskin session, he pulled into the parking lot of Clingan Ridge Baptist. He threw the car in park and hopped out. "I think you're ready to drive," he said. "Let's see if you can do it."

A few weeks earlier, the folks at Shepherd Center told me I shouldn't drive. They watched me improve for two full months, but I still had a long way to go. They concluded that my legs were too weak and my reaction time was too slow to get behind the wheel. To keep me from hurting myself or anyone else, they noted this in my discharge papers. Jeff, however, had seen me make significant strides. Besides, it was my vehicle. He didn't have anything to lose if I lost control and slammed into a light post or careened into a nearby tree.

I scooted over to the driver's seat, scared out of my wits. What would happen if I wrecked? Jeff pointed at the gearshift, crossed his arms, and relaxed. Could I do it? I eased off the brake to find out. The Explorer crept forward. I pressed the gas pedal, and the car sped up.

"Stop!"

I slammed on the brakes and white-knuckled the steering wheel. Jeff grinned. "Good job," he said. "Let's do it again."

I drove in circles in the parking lot for another ten minutes, stopping suddenly or slowly as Jeff directed. Then I pulled out of the parking lot and drove home. The drive was only a couple miles, but driving there felt like a miracle.

When I arrived home, Stacy's car was in the driveway. She often left work during lunch to eat in peace and quiet. I called her cell phone. "Come to the door," I said.

When she peeked out the door, I looked at her from the driver's seat with the biggest, goofiest grin in history. Every tooth showed. My eyes squinted to make more room for my smile to shine. Stacy, on the other hand, was not amused. A wisp of smoke issued from her ears. If looks could kill, Jeff and I would have died on the spot.

"Okay," Jeff whispered, careful not to mouth his move. "I'm leaving. You can walk yourself in."

In an instant, Jeff was out of the Explorer and inside his own car, backing toward safety. I was exposed and alone.

Stacy glared at me. "You could have died!" she screamed.

She was right. But I had to try it sometime, right? I had a goal, and I wasn't going to reach it with caution and a leisurely pace. I had a family to feed, and I needed to return to work. Otherwise, our cupboards would soon be bare, and I couldn't let that happen.

Chapter 11

Seeing God's Hand at Work

To be honest, my inspiration for walking and driving went beyond providing for my family. I had a twenty-foot Ranger bass boat, a nice home, a couple vehicles, and a heaping helping of pride. I didn't want to lose any of it. Sure, I could have stayed home and pulled a disability check, but I wanted to work. Besides, my time at the Shepherd Center showed me how blessed I was. I wasn't going to let those blessings go to waste.

That meant I needed to return to my previous job at the Cleveland Utilities wastewater plant. The job wasn't physically demanding, but stairs were everywhere. Five steps led to the front entrance. Three more steps led to a landing, and then twenty more reached up to my office.

I wasn't working an office job though. I spent most of my time down the hall from my office with the centrifuge.

The centrifuge spun solid and liquid waste at lightning speed, extracting as much water as possible. Once the waste was dewatered, I mixed in a polymer to turn the dry waste into a cake-like substance. This substance dropped into the bed of a dump truck. I then delivered the cake-like waste to a giant concrete pad, where it got taken by companies and used as class B sludge to fertilize crops.

Does the job stink? Smells like money to me.

Over the years, I transported countless loads of this cakey material, skipping up and down the stairs twenty-five times a day without a thought. Those carefree days were gone. Now, every stair was a threat. One wrong step, and I was face down, bloodied and bruised. If I was going to get my job back, I had to master the stairs. Fortunately, there were tools at Siskin to help regain my stair skills, and I used the tools to their maximum benefit.

In the middle of March 2010, I climbed six flights of Siskin stairs without stopping. My physical therapist had never seen anyone in my condition do that. She was so dazzled that she brought our time to an end. "I don't think you need us anymore," she said.

Elated, I called Tim Henderson, Safety Director at Cleveland Utilities. He met me at the wastewater plant's centrifuge building and videoed me climbing the stairs.

"Told you I could do it," I said. Tim nodded and congratulated me on my progress.

I was thrilled. Just a few months after a spinal cord injury, I relearned how to walk. Now, I was returning to work. I wasn't sure how I would manage the dump truck's manual transmission with my weak left foot, but I could climb stairs. I'd figure out the clutch on the job.

With video evidence of my stair-stepping ways, I headed to my primary care physician, Dr. Larry Swan. He gave me a once over and handed me a sealed letter, releasing me to relaunch my career. I handed the sealed letter to Jan Runyon in HR at Cleveland Utilities the next day. Jan tore the envelope open, then gave me a sad look. "Mark," she said, "this says you can't handle stairs."

I couldn't believe it—betrayed by my long-time doctor! Making matters worse, Dr. Swan was a Christian man who was committed to the truth. He was everything you want in a doctor. He even reached out to me while I was at Shepherd Center, stating that he and his staff were praying for me. Now he was sabotaging my efforts to reclaim my position at Cleveland Utilities. How could he?

I returned to Dr. Swan and forced him to change the letter. "I climbed six flights of stairs," I said. "It's in my notes from Siskin!"

He considered my plea and updated my release:

Can climb stairs in moderation.

It wasn't the wholehearted recommendation I hoped for, but I would make it work. When I showed the updated letter to Jan in HR, she picked up the phone and called the Vice President of Administration. "Rick," she said, "can you come to my office for a moment?" I wasn't sure why we needed Rick, but if he could help me get my job back, I was eager to see him.

Rick trotted into Jan's office and shook my hand. "Jan tells me you're ready to get back to work."

"I am," I said. "Tim's seen that I can climb stairs. I at

least want to give my old job a try."

Rick nodded, then slid a piece of paper across the desk to me. "How 'bout you consider this?"

It was a job description for a maintenance technician. Main responsibility: figuring out how much every piece of equipment cost the company over its lifetime of use. The position required no walking. There were no stairs to navigate and no clutch to stress over. It offered the same pay as my previous job.

"This is a desk job," I said, scanning the page. "Are you serious?"

"We're not taking pity on you," Rick said. "We think you're a perfect fit."

The position, I learned, was created two years earlier, right before the company entered into a hiring freeze. Because of the freeze, the job remained unfilled since its creation. The company's profits had since warmed up, and the freeze thawed. They were ready to fill the position.

"I'll take it!" I cried.

Rick laughed and pointed at the paper. "Not so fast," he said. "Take it home and talk to Stacy first."

There was nothing Stacy could say that would convince me to turn the job down. But I agreed to Rick's request. I took the paper home and showed it to Stacy. Together, we wondered at God's goodness and provision, that two years before I needed a new position, He put it in place.

————

On May 3, 2010—233 days after my accident, I headed to the corporate office for my first day as a maintenance technician. My coworkers threw a party for me, and even the Cleveland Utilities CEO attended. Many of these same coworkers visited me at Shepherd Center, and most doubted I would return. I was too frail, skinny, and weak the last time they saw me. Being with them again was a gift, and I wanted them to know the Giver.

"I don't know where your faith is," I said to the gathered crowd, "but God knew two years ago I would need this job. He goes before us and behind, taking care of us every step along our paths."

The party ended with hugs and handshakes. Afterward, I headed to my new office to learn how to use computerized management maintenance software, a.k.a. CMMS. It was a new program with potential that needed to be put to use. Some attempted to use it previously with negative results. So, they abandoned the software, hoping someone else would come along to figure it out. I was that someone else.

With no one to train me, I spent day after day tinkering with the program, trying one thing and then another. I gained ground, but it was a slow, painful process. It felt like rehab all over again. Every step forward came with two steps backward. Eventually, the breakthroughs outweighed the setbacks, and I understood the software well enough to produce useful information. I once again felt like an asset instead of a liability.

That feeling of usefulness stopped at the curb outside of corporate headquarters. It was a low curb, but it presented a risk, threatening my balance every time I entered or left the building. The threat didn't last long though. Soon after my return, upper management asked how they could make my life easier. I mentioned the curb. Without hesitation, they installed a ramp.

The company could have let me go. Every step I took represented a liability, but they cared for me and worked hard to keep me part of the team. The gesture humbles me to this day. Unfortunately, they couldn't protect me from every adversary.

Walking toward the front entrance one winter day, I noticed a frozen snail. The little guy probably struggled for hours to get across the sidewalk the night before, but he wasn't fast enough. The freezing temperature stopped him in his tracks. I felt sorry for the fellow and tried to lift my left foot high enough to avoid stepping on him. It didn't work.

My foot caught on his stiff body. Lacking the balance to compensate, I hit the ground hard. The snail didn't move an inch. I got back to my feet with scraped palms, a bruised ego, and a commitment to never feel sorry for another snail as long as I live.

———————

Five years after starting my new position, CMMS was no longer a mystery. It was a beneficial software program producing useful data that saved the company a lot of money. I'd gone through countless trials and experienced plenty of errors, but the software functioned as it should.

Feeling a sense of accomplishment, I was ready to exchange CMMS management for a new challenge. A retiring lab analyst offered the opportunity I sought.

Working in the lab would let me use my science background, as I weighed and analyzed water samples. On the residential side, I'd ensure drinking water had a proper amount of fluoride—not too much, not too little. Then I would have commercial responsibilities, certifying that water discharged from local businesses had acceptably low levels of bacteria and metals. The goal was that every drop of water that entered the Hiwassee River was cleaner than the river itself.

I got the gig.

The lab's in a one-level building at the wastewater treatment plant, where another curb blocked my entry. Administrators noticed the problem and turned a section of the curb into a ramp—another reason to give thanks.

———

Years after my initial return to work, I realized how foolhardy my plan was to return to my previous position. Sure, I could climb six sets of stairs in a rehabilitation setting. But could I run up and down twenty-eight stairs multiple times a day and wrestle the dump truck's manual transmission into submission? There's no way. I would have tapped out after two days.

Fortunately, God knew my limits better than I did, and He provided a job that worked around them.

Chapter 12

PSA: People Need People

It SOUNDS SILLY, BUT FOR most of my life, I didn't realize people used wheelchairs. I mean, I knew people used wheelchairs, but I never noticed the people using wheelchairs. They may as well have been invisible.

Now, I see people in wheelchairs everywhere I look. While they spend more time than most thinking about stairs, the width of door openings, and the height of food items at the store, they're pretty much the same as everyone else. They have hopes and dreams, loves and fears. They need help, and they don't like asking for it.

What made the difference in my perspective? The answer seems obvious, but I'll explain.

Before my injury, I felt self-sufficient. If I needed something done, I didn't ask for help. I just did it.

Case in point: Before leaving for our ill-fated trip

to Savannah, Stacy and I built a fence around our pool. Together, we dug post holes, dropped eight-foot-long four-by-fours into place, leveled and balanced fence panels, and hung gates. It was grueling work that dragged on one week after another. The end result was a functional fence that guaranteed no one accidentally wound up in our pool.

While the fence looked great, Stacy shouldn't have been out there helping me. Before you label me a sexist, hear me out. I understand that women can dig holes and build fences. Remember—I recruited my wife to do just that. But I also coached a fifteen-member men's softball team, and I know that every man on that team would have cherished the opportunity to lend a hand. If I'd thought to ask them, they would have built the fence with joy and speed. (Generally speaking, lots of people get things done quicker than two people.)

However, I didn't ask for help. Didn't even think about asking. If the thought had crossed my mind, I probably would have dismissed it and built the fence myself anyway. Stacy and I were healthy and able-bodied, and while building a fence takes time and sweat, it's a fairly easy task. Besides, I didn't want to bother anyone or seem needy by asking for help.

In retrospect, I see that was a mistake. I should have asked for help—not just for the fence, but for all kinds of projects. Instead, I handled the tasks on my own. It seemed like the right thing to do. But was it?

———————

Whether you're turning screws or raking leaves, pulling Christmas ornaments out of the attic or building a chicken coop, something magical happens when you work alongside someone. You may labor in silence for hours, but that silence doesn't last forever. Eventually, a dam breaks. One of you opens up. Something's going on, and one of you needs to talk about it. A restoration project transforms into a therapy session, or the work site becomes a safe place to share victories and defeats.

I should know. The one time I asked for help on a major project changed my life.

Early in my marriage to Stacy, we felt called to adopt teenage girls. After a state-mandated eleven-week education course, we were ready. Our home just needed some adjusting. Stacy and I planned to build a bedroom in our basement for the young lady we hoped to adopt.

I headed to Lowe's for supplies. As I scanned the aisles, I saw Eric Clements, a maintenance man at Cleveland Utilities. I barely knew the guy, but I knew he had skills I needed. We went through the typical pleasantries before I got down to business. "Are we friends?" I asked.

He looked at me like I had three eyes, then replied that yes, we were friends. I followed his response with a second question: "Would you be interested in helping me finish part of my basement?"

He looked at me strangely again. I explained what Stacy and I had in mind and why. With my most effective puppy-dog eyes, I guilted Eric into the project.

Two months later, the basement was ready for a new resident, and I had a new friend—a true friend, someone who later partnered with me during fishing tournaments, visited me while recovering from my spinal injury, and cried with me in the driveway when I returned home from Shepherd Center. It all started with a request for help, which resulted in hours spent side by side, talking about anything and everything while we framed, drywalled, and mudded a basement bedroom.

Sadly, that was one of the few times I requested or accepted such help. Most of the time, I closed myself off to the opportunity. Because I could do things on my own, I did. So, I didn't experience the ministry of being present. My pride robbed me of the chance to be a listening ear or find a listening ear, to help someone process highs or lows, to lift others or be lifted up by others in prayer. I traded those fellowship opportunities for a perceived self-reliance.

I now realize it was all a sham. People need people, regardless of physical ability or mental acuity.

Today, my need for others is obvious. Without the aid of loved ones, I can't do half the stuff I need to do. But the truth is, I needed people before the accident just as much as I need them now. I just couldn't see it until the accident made it painfully, permanently clear.

Years after my accident, I can't stay on my feet for prolonged periods or use an extension ladder. I suspect I can military press 1,000 pounds* while on my knees,

---

Okay, 1,000 pounds may be an exaggeration, but you get the point.

but I tumble over if I try to pick up a two-pound box from a standing position. It takes longer to get dressed, to shower, to walk to the car. Mowing grass is the only thing I don't do slowly. Inspired by my brother's race history and a desire to make up for every other task that now takes longer to complete, I drive my zero-turn mower like a lunatic, leaving a trail of smoke behind me as I break land speed records with every new line shaved in the yard.

Why am I writing about this? Because someone—you, perhaps—needs to hear it. All of us start life in diapers, and we'll finish in diapers as well. Some of us just get a head start. And our diapers aren't just physical. They're emotional, spiritual, mental. We're handicapped by selfishness and pride, greed, and—in America, especially—a rugged determinism and individualism that convinces us we can do life on our own.

Hard truth: We can't make it through life alone.

Motivational truth: That's okay. We were created that way.

Admitting we need help connects us to each other and builds community. When one person asks for help, it encourages others to reach out when they're in need. Asking for help gives people the opportunity to love their neighbors (that's you), to connect in ways they were created for.

Some people are master carpenters, and others are prayer warriors. Some people can quilt gorgeous blankets, and others can play the flute or guitar. Some people are great storytellers, and others are great listeners.

Whoever you are, whatever your gifts, you need me,

and I need you. We all need one another, and we can all help each other.

With that in mind, use your gifts, large and small. When you do, you show the world an unusual love—a love that gives without expectation, a love like that of our Savior.

Chapter 13

Ole Slew Foot

CHRISTIANS THROUGHOUT HISTORY HAVE
BATTLED Ole Slew Foot.* I'm no exception.

During my tenure as a Sunday school teacher, I
was plagued with doubt. I often felt inadequate and
underprepared. On one hand, this was understandable.
Teaching adult Sunday school was a heavy responsibility.
Students read and studied the Bible on their own. If I
didn't know my stuff and missed the mark, someone
would correct me. There's nothing wrong with a loving
correction, but if a teacher makes a habit of getting things
wrong—especially the essentials, it's time to look for a
new teacher.

Ole Slew Foot took advantage of this truth and twisted
it to his own devilish end.

Ole Slew Foot is a Southern nickname for Lucifer or Satan.

You're not good enough.
You're not smart enough.
You shouldn't be leading a class.

He repeated the refrain in my ear time and again. Eventually, he didn't have to say anything. I took the lead, my brain insisting I was a fish out of water, that God couldn't use someone like me. Or at least He shouldn't.

This rang true, because I wasn't the ideal Sunday school teacher. I'd been out of church for years, and the only reason I returned was Stacy—a girl I had a crush on in elementary school.

When I first noticed her, she was in third grade, a year younger than me. But age didn't put a damper on my feelings. A friend thought my secret infatuation was funny, so he teased me with a custom song that borrowed the title character's name from the 1970's television series *Marcus Welby*:

Marcus Welby here,
To see his little dear:
Stacy.

Twenty years later, when Stacy walked into Cooke's Food Store, my elementary friend's song rang in my head—*Marcus Welby here*. I called out to get Stacy's attention. She walked a few more paces, then paused. I don't know if it was curiosity or an ancient memory from elementary school, but she turned around. After a few minutes of catching up, I asked her out.

"I have two sons," she said.

"Bring them with you."

That night, Stacy, her two sons, and I dined together at McDonald's, the boys' favorite eatery. As if that didn't set the bar high enough, I followed this with a trip to the local fire station. Since I was a volunteer firefighter, I had access to the station anytime I wanted. The boys were in childhood heaven, as they sat in the front seat of a real-life fire truck and imagined themselves rushing away to save the day. I turned on the overhead lights, and they looked at me like I were a superhero. I felt like one, too.

A few months earlier, I'd graduated from the University of Tennessee at Chattanooga with my education degree. Now, I was entertaining two boys I barely knew and courting their mother, whom I had a crush on in elementary school. That's superhero stuff, if you ask me.

Stacy and I got a few more dates under our belts in the coming weeks. Then our blossoming relationship led me to attend Clingan Ridge Baptist Church, where Stacy was a member. I'd not been to church in a while, but the lingo and environment were familiar. I paid attention to the sermons, sang the songs with gusto, and asked questions during Sunday school. A few months into my renewed church attendance, the Sunday school teacher suggested I take over his class.

"Give me the information, and I'll teach it," I said.

My answer should have been a red flag. *Give me the information*? The information was in the Bible, but I didn't know that. The teacher overlooked that minor flaw and that fall, I was elected to teach the class.

Thankfully, I wasn't left to my own devices. Lifeway published a commentary series that helped keep me on track. This was vital, as I obviously wasn't equipped to teach anyone about the Bible.

Such issues didn't faze my Baptist brothers or God. Their confidence encouraged me to do my best. I dove into the Scripture, eager to understand the material so I could handle any potential questions that arose during class. Because God's Word does not return void, this digging did a work on my heart. God used my studies to convict me of sin and show me corners of my life that conflicted with His heart. I began making changes—developing relationships I'd long neglected and applying myself to learning more about God. As I did, I saw that there weren't just nooks and crannies in my life that lacked God's touch. Every area was in need.

Teaching Sunday school, which started as a potential mistake, led to a new flourishing. I was becoming the man God created me to be. Yet the closer I drew to God, the louder Ole Slew Foot's voice grew. The accuser insisted I was incompetent and unworthy. I knew Satan was a liar, but it was hard to ignore his running commentary. Thanks to the wisdom of my brothers and sisters at Clingan Ridge Baptist, I kept Satan's feedback at bay and continued teaching the class and moving toward Christ and right thinking.

When I surrendered my teaching post more than a decade later, the doubts returned. *You shouldn't have been teaching in the first place. Who do you think you are?* Then

God showed me the truth. He had used my teaching assignment to pull me out of ignorance and draw me closer to Him. He used Scripture and the great cloud of witnesses to overcome my inadequacies.

As I listened to God's voice, Satan's faded. But Ole Slew Foot wasn't through with me. That horrific ride on the Nauti Dawg gave him new fodder. At any given moment after the accident, I was liable to hear Slew's taunts:

> *God doesn't really love you. If He did, He wouldn't let this happen. God doesn't let those He loves go through such suffering.*

The Bible has answers to these accusations. It's filled with examples that prove these claims are bold-faced lies, that God's chosen people have suffered for generations, and those who loved Him most often suffered extraordinarily. Paul endured persecution and an unspecified "thorn in the flesh." Jeremiah experienced such sadness that he penned an entire book, Lamentations, to document it. Job watched his wealth, health, family, and friends either disappear before his eyes or turn on him. David, whom God labeled "a man after His own heart," was under frequent threat and forced to run for his life. And Jesus, the third person in the Trinity, King of kings and Lord of lords, lived as an outcast and died on a tree like a cursed, common criminal.

Even with the bulk of evidence against his claims, Ole Slew Foot puts up effective arguments. He did it to me, particularly in the early weeks and months after my accident. Any assurance that God loved me was painstakingly inspected. When held up to the light of experience and the world's standards, God's love came up short. I read that God uses all things for the good of those who love Him, but I couldn't see how a ruined fishing trip and permanent disability could be used for my good. This sent me to dark places. Were it not for people who loved me and pointed me toward Jesus, I may have stayed in the dark. Satan would have won.

As the appropriately popularized sentence fragment goes, *But God . . .*

God graciously protected me from that dark fate. He lifted my eyes to see His glory, reminding me that love doesn't always look like good health, mobility, and independence, but it always looks like sacrifice. He reminded me of this through family and friends. And of those who sacrificed on my behalf, none outdid Stacy. She gave up her normal, small-town life to live with and love a broken man with a laundry list of needs. When I was down, she comforted me, reminding me that God was faithful and—despite what we could see with our eyes—He was using my injury for my good and His glory.

All would be well, because God loved me. So did Stacy.

"I love you more today than I did before the accident." Stacy squeezed my arm, as if to verify the words were true. I didn't need verbal confirmation. Her actions said it all. Ever since the accident, Stacy showed her love in an increasing number of practical ways. While I laid around at the house recovering, she made sure I had food to eat and that my phone was nearby and charged. When we went to Lowe's or the mall, she pushed me in my wheelchair through parking lots and aisles. She never complained that I took longer to complete basic tasks.

These loving actions spoke to me, and they left me hurting for Stacy. I knew life with me wasn't easy. I was needy in ways that few people experience, and she was on the front lines of meeting those needs.

Adjusting to post-accident life was one of many trials we faced in our marriage. Since our wedding on November 11, 1997, a string of obstacles blocked our access to calm and peace. Some of it was expected. Stacy was a divorced mother of two, and I was a bachelor stepping into the role of stepdad. Read enough books or watch enough movies, and you know this is a recipe for drama.

Things heated up as the boys aged. Their acting out brought increased heartache and consequences, as Matthew dabbled in temporary homelessness and Travis impregnated a neighbor.

Through it all, our marriage thrived. Whatever came our way, our relationship took the hits and kept going. Yet even with Stacy's assurances that her love remained steady, I wondered if she regretted our union. When we wed, the whole "sickness or health" thing was hypothetical, confined to cold and flu viruses and the eventual decay that comes with old age. She didn't sign up for this.

I repeated my offer out of sympathy. "You can leave," I told her on regular occasions, "and I would understand."

She never flinched at the proposition. She wasn't leaving, so—she insisted—I could stop asking.

By the spring of 2014, we were in a new two-story house. The boys, now in their early twenties, lived on their own. We were five years past the accident and well-adjusted to our new norm. Anyone who looked at our marriage from the outside would have been impressed. I was impressed with our marriage, and I had the best seat in the house—smack-dab in the middle of it all.

That's why I was so surprised when Stacy hit me with the news. She looked me in the eyes, as the evening sun reflected off the floors, and said, "I'm leaving."

Chapter 14

Signs & Symptoms of a Dying Marriage

It was the ultimate blindside.

We loved each other, followed Jesus together, and successfully stomped through more than our fair share of life's thicks and thins. Other couples had problems and separated—not us. We didn't fuss at each other or fight. Neither of us abused the other physically, emotionally, or otherwise. There were no cracks in our marriage, no signs pointing toward divorce. Or were there?

————

Sometimes, Stacy had a hard time sleeping. Her remedy was to play games on her iPad. One of her favorites was Golf Solitaire. I rolled over many nights to see Stacy's face lit up by the iPad's glow, as she worked toward a new high score.

One night, I rolled over and noticed something different. Stacy wasn't moving electronic playing cards around the screen. She was replying to a coworker's text.

I love you, too.

I should have asked Stacy whom she loved. A normal husband would have, but I didn't give it a second thought. Sleep was calling. More importantly, there was no reason to be suspicious. Stacy told everyone she met that she loved them. It didn't matter who it was or how close they were. Stacy loved all people. To see that a coworker wrote *I love you* and that Stacy replied *I love you, too* didn't set off any alarms. Everyone loved Stacy, and she loved them in return.

I saw that love in action. Every time I attended one of Stacy's work functions, coworkers surrounded Stacy, eager to give her a hug and thank her for being a great boss. They looked up to Stacy, and she took good care of them. It was a joy to watch her admirers, knowing I had a more special relationship with her than any of them.

So, seeing my wife send a text that she loved someone else wasn't abnormal. It was par for the course.

With no impression that the text thread had romantic implications, I closed my eyes and fell asleep.

––––––––––

"But you don't look like a boy!"

Stacy turned sideways to offer counterargument. No matter what way she turned, she looked shapely, womanly. But my opinion didn't matter. She didn't believe me when I told her she was beautiful, that I was tickled to have her by my side and didn't see a thing wrong with her. She wanted a tummy tuck, leg liposuction, and breast lift and augmentation, and she would pay for it herself if that's what it took.

While I didn't see the need for any of it, I wasn't going to let my wife foot the bill for her Total Mommy Makeover. We were married. What was mine was hers, and that included my wallet. It was my job to provide for my family, even if the requested provision didn't make sense to me. I told her to get the makeover if it would make her feel better, and I'd pay.

"Are you going to take care of me while I recover?" she asked.

I tried to imagine what recovery from cosmetic surgery entailed. "I'm going to try."

My offer was put to the test a few weeks later, and I did all I could to fulfill my end of the bargain. I brought Stacy food and her iPad and phone, cleaned the fluid-catching bulbs on either side of her stomach, and helped her get to the bathroom. I welcomed her female coworkers who showed up to encourage her along the road to healing. I did it all while avoiding my greatest fear—losing my balance and falling on top of my recovering wife.

Stacy looked at me with appreciation. "You've done a great job," she said. "I didn't think you would take care of me this well."

"I didn't think I'd be able to," I admitted.

The tables had turned. After years of being cared for, I was the caregiver, even if in a limited capacity. Our conversations were light and playful, and our home felt happy.

A few days into recovery, Mom brought food over and asked for a peek at Stacy's modified physique. Stacy raised her shirt for Mom's inspection. Mom looked on in appreciation.

"I'm sorry," Stacy said after lowering her shirt. "For everything."

Mom grinned. "It's okay," she said. "None of us knew what was going on at the Shepherd Center. We all made mistakes."

Stacy thanked Mom for understanding. Mom said goodbye and left Stacy to enjoy the bowl of chicken and dumplings with a side of forgiveness.

A week later, Stacy broke the news. She was leaving the marriage and leaving me with the $18,000 bill for her Total Mommy Makeover.

––––––––

I realize how this looks. I'm writing the book and get to cast someone else as the villain in my marriage. I know it takes two people to make a relationship work and two to make it fail. Surely I played a role in the divorce, right?

After running my marriage through countless postmortems, I've concluded that I could have been a better husband. I spent a lot of time in the woods and on the water, hunting and fishing. I could have spent that time at home with Stacy, talking about life, studying the Bible, or doing a million other things.

That said, if my hobbies were the source of our marital woes, Stacy never told me. She frequently joined me on the boat for a day of fishing. While she didn't hunt with me, she never complained when I went. She spent those days hanging out with her sister or friends or at home with her sons, scrapbooking to her heart's content. I don't recall her ever asking me to spend less time on my hobbies. If she had, I would have responded positively. At least I hope I would have. We'll never know, because she never gave me the chance.

———

With our divorce pending, I hunted for any chance at reconciliation. I threw myself at Stacy's feet and offered to go to couple's counseling.

"Your mom and dad are counselors," she said. "I don't trust any of them."

"Pick the counselor—someone out of town," I suggested, "and we'll go. I'll go alone if that's what you want. Whatever it takes, I'll do it."

"No."

"Is there anything I can do—anything at all?"

"No."

Stacy was adamant. I was heartbroken and confused,

stuck at a dead end with no direction, no clue how to move forward with life when the life I loved was falling apart.

I called my parents and told them the news. Their hurt oozed through the phone. Even with the lingering pain from the Shepherd Center ordeal, my parents loved Stacy. They didn't want to lose her. At the end of our call, Mom asked if she could let Jamie know. "Sure," I said. "Won't hurt anything."

An hour later, Jamie was in my living room, balancing a laptop on his knees. I gave him the username and password to my cell phone plan. He downloaded a list of phone numbers Stacy called, placed them on a spreadsheet, and ran them through a script. One number showed up more than any other.

"That's him." Jamie pointed at ten digits on the screen. "That's who she's having an affair with."

An affair?

I looked at the call log. Stacy called the number earlier that morning. My stomach lurched. There was a reason for the divorce—a real, flesh-and-blood reason. A few more keystrokes, and Jamie had a name. Facebook gave us a face. The source of my impending divorce worked for Stacy and grew up down the street from me.

When Stacy came home that afternoon, she brushed past me and changed out of her work clothes. I followed her. She acted coy and uncomfortable to have me, her husband, watch her change. I decided to match her Oscar-worthy performance. I'd seen her act before, and she was good. Very good.

Every Halloween, Clingan Ridge Baptist put on Judgement House, a scare-the-Hell-out-of-you event. Stacy and I volunteered to help one year and were given the role of parents. The story was simple: Our son was in a car wreck and wasn't going to survive. When the nurse told us the news, we were supposed to act distraught.

Stacy went above and beyond the call of duty, crying actual tears and calling out to God for help. It had a powerful effect on those who watched. It had less of an effect on Stacy.

As soon as a group of event-goers left the room, Stacy wiped her face and joked around. She did this over and over, turning on the water works at will and shutting them off just as easily. Her skill was impressive. It was also unnerving.

Standing face to face, confronting her about our impending divorce, I wondered if Stacy's acting skills would be on display. "You sure there's nobody we can talk to—maybe a friend or—"

"No," she said.

"No counselors or friends?" I stuffed my hands in my pockets. "What about"—I inhaled slowly—"Derek?"

Stacy's eyes bulged, a deer caught in headlights. Then she gave me a piece of her mind.

Any satisfaction I received from my gotcha moment dissolved. I was devastated, unsure how to function without my wife of seventeen years, my anchor who saw me through my darkest, most difficult days and asked for nothing that my broken body and soul couldn't provide.

I yearned for her to change her mind, to put the brakes

on the divorce and restore our marriage. I was ready to forgive her, to welcome her back with open arms, to put her infidelity in the rearview mirror and move forward. If given the chance, I would have suffered a second broken back if it meant keeping my marriage intact.

My reasons weren't all holy and pious. The impending loneliness was too much to bear. Who would take me—a divorced paraplegic?

"We can get through this," I said. "I'm willing to forgive you."

She shook her head. "I've got to do this, for myself."

"Stacy!" I threw my hands up. "Do you know how selfish that sounds? You know what you're doing and what the Word of God says about it. Please . . ."

"I have to do this for me."

With that, she walked away, putting an end to the conversation. But it wasn't the last talk we had on the topic. While she was ready to cut me out of her life, she didn't have a place to stay. For nearly a month, we cohabitated under one roof, moving toward divorce and forced to share space.

I slept in our master suite, and she crashed in an upstairs bedroom like an out-of-town visitor.

I didn't attempt to hide my pain. Every time we crossed paths at home, I cried. "Are you sure we can't work it out?" I begged. "Can't we just try?"

Her answer was always the same: "No." Sometimes, she accented it with something extra: "This is still my house. As soon as I get my stuff out of here, I'll be gone."

————

Eventually, Stacy's dad and brother came to haul her belongings away, amplifying the awkwardness ten-fold. They barely looked at me and didn't utter a word, moving Stacy's stuff in silence. After a few minutes of proximal discomfort, I scurried into my bedroom to escape two men I loved for nearly twenty years.

The move only took half an hour. When the shuffling feet shuffled out of the house, I stepped back into the living room. Stacy left all the furniture and electronics. She didn't take a single piece of our bedroom suite. She didn't fight for anything, letting me keep the house and all my retirement earnings. There was only one thing she wanted: an easy way out of our marriage.

She got it.

The divorce was fast tracked. Stacy had no demands, which meant no lengthy court arguments. Her lack of interest surprised me. At the time, I was in a legal battle to earn compensation for my spinal injury. If I won, I could have caught a windfall worth millions.* Stacy didn't care. She didn't want any of it.

Thanks to Stacy's indifference, we showed up at court, signed some papers, and that was it. With the stroke of a pen, on July 24, 2014, Stacy and I drained the final drops of life from our seventeen-year marriage. Cause of death: *Irreconcilable differences*. To my knowledge, the

————

I didn't get millions from the lawsuit. Actually, I didn't get a penny. Sigh . . .

only difference between the two of us was that one of us wanted to stay married and the other did not. That difference, however, was ultimately irreconcilable.

Simple as the divorce proceedings were, the aftermath was a complicated pool of confusion and pain. While I grieved daily, no one suffered more than our grandson, Jaden.

Over the years, Stacy and I often cared for Jaden. Our home was a haven, a needed place of stability in Jaden's otherwise volatile life. With Stacy gone, that stability was undermined, our once-happy home remodeled into a house haunted by the past and occupied by a lone, lonely paraplegic.

I wasn't the best granddad, but I tried. I had to. When Stacy walked away from me, she also abandoned her sons and grandson. For years, I carried the parent and grandparent mantles on my own, keeping Jaden and helping Travis when I could. But it wasn't the same. Despite the math of it all, one grandparent is not half as effective as two, especially when the remaining grandparent relies on a cane and can't pick up a crying child without toppling over.

Miraculously, I wouldn't be on my own forever. God had big plans once again.

Chapter 15

From Ghostwriter to Marriage Material

As USUAL, THE WAITING ROOM of Dr. Swan's office bordered on standing room only.

I filled out the obligatory paperwork and showed my license and insurance card before plopping down in a cushioned seat. To my left, the owners of Cooke's Food Store posed on the cover of *GoodNews* magazine, a free Christian publication that featured stories from local writers. I grabbed the magazine and flipped its pages, looking for something that grabbed my attention.

Near the back was a poem titled "I Know What It Feels Like." Four small butterflies danced on the page, and the poem's first line spoke to me.

I know what it feels like to be sad, so I give them a smile.

I didn't know to whom the author gifted smiles, but I knew sadness.

I know what it feels like to be lonely, so I give them friendship.

Another lonely soul? And she used her pain for the good of others?

I know what it feels like to need encouragement . . . to want someone to love me . . . to be scared . . . to hurt . . . [to] want someone to reach out to me . . .

Line after line struck my heart and filled me with a sense of connection. There was someone else out there like me, someone who had been battered and bruised by life. Yet somehow, this person had nothing but generosity to show for it. She also had a way with words, something I lost with the divorce.

Months earlier, I started writing a book. I wanted to share about my accident and how I came to understand God's faithfulness in the midst of difficult situations. The book was my way of making sense of what happened and sharing God's goodness with the world. It was also a way to thank Stacy for her love through the twists and turns in our story.

I was a few chapters into the story when Stacy dropped the D bomb. Like that, all my momentum vanished. I'd not written a word since. It hurt too much to relive the past by writing about it in an empty house, but I still felt the story should be told. Perhaps this stranger, this poet, could ghostwrite my book.

A short bio at the bottom of the page stated that the author taught at Black Fox Elementary and could be reached on Facebook. I scanned the poem to discern whether it was a good idea to contact the author or a sign of insanity. The butterflies convinced me it was safe, so I messaged the writer on Facebook. She responded that she would love to hear my testimony.

How do you want to do that? I wrote. *You want to meet or talk on the phone?*

————————

I sat on the entryway bench at Jordan's BBQ as Kelly walked in. I'd seen her photo in *GoodNews* and on Facebook, but the pictures did her beauty no justice. I stuttered my way through an introduction, and our waitress led us to a table.

We ordered loaded baked potatoes and spent a few minutes on small talk. Then Kelly asked about my story. I gave an abbreviated version and asked if she'd be interested in helping me get the whole thing down in my book.

"I have a better idea," she said. "You should write for *GoodNews*."

It wasn't what I expected, but it was an appealing offer. The stories in the magazine were 500 words, much less intimidating than writing a whole book. I said I would think about it, then asked Kelly to share her story. She started in, just as someone behind her turned to face me. It was an old friend from Clingan Ridge Baptist. I'd moved churches years before, but he didn't care. He was just glad to see me happy. He nodded toward Kelly and gave me a thumbs-up.

I couldn't tell him this was a lunch meeting, not a date. Kelly had started telling her story, and I didn't want to interrupt. The guy should have known this wasn't romantic. My divorce finalized three months earlier, and my head was too garbled to consider finding a new wife, especially one with kids. Falling in love with a mother of two was a story I was all too familiar with, and it didn't end well the first time. I'd be a fool to do it a second time.

Then again, she was mighty pretty.

"I love my kids," Kelly said as she told of her past. I wanted to believe her, but anyone could say they loved their kids. The proof was in the pudding, and I'd not gotten a taste of it yet. But I enjoyed our lunchtime barbecue and wondered if I would eventually see how much she loved her kids with my own eyes.

We met for a couple more fact-finding meetings before easing into a dating relationship. The two most important people in Kelly's life—her fifteen-year-old son, Codey, and twelve-year-old daughter, Gracie—had no idea I existed. Kelly wanted it that way. In fact, she demanded it stay that way. Her kids experienced a lot of heartache in their first few years of life, and it took ongoing, intentional effort to build and maintain an environment of peace and safety. Kelly didn't want to upset their world again by introducing some random guy who messaged her on Facebook. Especially since there was no reason to believe I would be around for the long haul.

Though she hid our relationship from her kids, Kelly let others in on our romance, honing her private investigator chops in the process. She contacted her friends at Clingan Ridge Baptist, asking all about this handsome Mark fellow who stole her heart at first sight. (Note: Part of that last sentence may be a stretch, but remember—this is my story, so I tell it my way.) Whatever my church friends said worked. Kelly didn't run away.

While I didn't meet Kelly's kids for a few months, I found out firsthand that Kelly put them first. We often talked on the phone in the evenings—a supplement to our sporadic, covert dates. No matter what we were talking about, our conversations always got cut short at bedtime. "I'll call you back in an hour, hour and a half," Kelly said, night after night. I waited for those late-night calls with a light heart and heavy eyelids, excited to continue our conversations that brought joy in the moment and lethargy in the morning.

Our secret relationship went public when Kelly accepted an invitation to dinner at my house.

I opened the door to Kelly's smile, Codey's poker face, and Gracie's burning hatred. I served homemade pinto beans, fried potatoes, and cornbread. Everyone ate with pleasure, even though Gracie did her best to hide it. I let Codey drive my zero-turn mower around the yard and taught him to tie a fly for fishing. I pulled out all the stops, and I thought I moved the needle in a positive direction.

I was wrong.

There was no room for me. For years, Gracie and Codey had their mother all to themselves. They shared a unique history and were bound together by trauma and faith. Ever since Kelly kicked her ex-husband out of the house years earlier, Codey had been the man of the house, the protector of the castle. He had no interest in giving up his post to a stranger. If he knew my house payment and credit card bill kept my bank account hovering between four cents and ten dollars, his suspicion of me would have grown, and he would have kicked me to the curb. Thankfully, he didn't know about my financial woes. Even a light kick from his size-eleven boots would have knocked me to the ground.

I was disheartened at the kids' response, but I didn't give up. Kelly's love for her Savior and her children attracted me as much as her sweet smile, and I could see a future with her. Getting there would just take time.

Eager to reach that future, I asked Kelly out on more dates. Sometimes she accepted, other times she declined. In an eighteen-month period, she broke off our relationship half a dozen times, every rejection punctuated with the same excuse: "It's hard on the kids."

I didn't give up. Instead, I brainstormed ways to weasel my way back into Kelly's life. I sent texts and Facebook messages to remind her of my existence. When she gave me permission to re-enter her life, I went out of my way to avoid the next breakup. That included appeals to Gracie and Codey. I openly admitted I didn't deserve their mom and insisted I would do my best to take care of her. They side-eyed me, but my persistence began to wear them down. Little by little, their icy hearts thawed toward me. They let me join them on family outings and take them on local adventures. On rare occasions, they even smiled.

I grew to love Kelly more each day. I watched in awe as she interacted with Codey and Gracie, inspired by one thought: *If I can con her into loving me like she loves those kids, I'll be set for life.*

While I played the long game to win Kelly's heart, I took her advice and pitched an article to *GoodNews* magazine, a 500-word version of my testimony. They accepted and published the story in the January issue. With the New Year on my brain, I titled the story "New Steps for a New Year." This publishing experience encouraged me to write more.

For a while, I submitted a story every month, often tying my topic to a holiday. February's article was titled "My Soul Mate." When I showed Kelly the headline, she thought I was off my rocker. We'd just started dating, and I was already talking about being soul mates. Or so she thought. The article wasn't a love letter to her. It was a recommendation that readers run to God, their true soul mate and one chance at unconditional love. Kelly relaxed. I wasn't as crazy as she suspected.

––––––––––

As the kids warmed to me, I wormed my way deeper into their lives until I was spending every available hour with Kelly, Gracie, and Codey. If I wasn't at their house, they were at mine. I could see a light at the end of the tunnel, and it featured a preacher and wedding rings. It was time to test the waters.

We were at my house, and Kelly was in the living room. I walked out of the kitchen with a hand behind my back. Kelly leapt to her feet and held out both hands like a traffic guard. "Don't you do it," she said. "Mark, I'm not kidding—don't you do it!"

"What's wrong?" I brought out my hidden hand from behind my back, which held a grape Ring Pop still in the wrapper. "It's just candy. What did you think it was?"

Test results were negative. Kelly wasn't ready for the big question. I laughed it off, and we went on with our day. But I wondered if and when she would be ready. We'd been dating in sporadic intervals for a year, and I was eager to take the next step. I hoped she would be ready soon. Until then, I was forced to wait.

Thankfully, the waiting didn't last too long. In a remarkable turn of events, Gracie and Codey—my one-time nemeses and the reason Kelly dumped me repeatedly—became my greatest advocates. They were impressed with my stick-to-itiveness, stubbornness, or whatever quality kept me coming back for more after the breakups. They liked something else even more. When I promised to do something, I did it.

I loved Kelly and the kids. Maybe I wasn't the big, bad wolf Codey and Gracie initially feared. And maybe it was time for Kelly to seal the deal.

"What are you waiting for?" Codey and Gracie asked

their mother. "Just marry the guy!"

Blessing of blessings, Kelly listened to her children.

Making it to the wedding date took some lifestyle changes. When we got engaged,[*] I was living paycheck to paycheck, attempting to maintain a two-income lifestyle on a single income. I wanted something in my savings account before we got married. So, I sold the house and did what every adult dreads. I moved in with my parents.

For six months, I was back under my parents' roof. Horrific as it sounds, it was a wonderful time to reconnect with my parents in a new, more consistent manner. Knowing the move was temporary made it even better.

Eighteen months after our first official date, Kelly and I took advantage of a low-cost elopement package at Overlook Inn on Fort Mountain and wed on March 21, 2016. We haven't broken up since.

————

To put it simply, Kelly is a gift, the best thing to ever happen to me. She loves sincerely and fully with a single-minded devotion. Gracie and Codey—the finest kids in the galaxy—are icing on the cake. In addition to their other attributes, they love me and care for me with a generosity that blows me away.

Exhibit A: Codey and I sat side by side in a cramped

————

Because I'm a hopeless romantic who loves Kelly, Codey, and Gracie, I chose an engagement ring with three stones. The larger one in the middle is for Kelly, and the smaller flanking stones are for Codey and Gracie.

shooting house near the Hiwassee River. After three days of sitting, we'd not seen a single white tail. The sun dipped near the horizon, bringing on dusk. It would soon be too dark to see.

Just then, a doe walked across the right side of our shelter. Codey and I agreed earlier that I'd handle anything on the right side, and he'd take the left. Codey said, "Take the shot."

I sat up in my backless chair and did what now comes so naturally to me. I lost my balance. Before I hit the ground or dropped my gun, Codey's strong hand grabbed hold of my shirt back. With Codey holding me steady, I raised my rifle, took aim, and shot.

We waited a few minutes before tracking the deer. When we found it, we realized we'd made a mistake. It wasn't a doe. It was a button buck—a young male deer with undeveloped antlers. The kill was legal, but problematic. My family has pride, so we only harvest male deer with eight or more points. This one didn't have a single point. Sneaking the deer home was going to be tough. My brother-in-law and a friend were on the hunt with us, stationed 200 yards away.

Codey and I left the deer, crept to the truck, and settled on a story and a plan.

When the rest of our party arrived, they were empty-handed. I lied and said we didn't even see a deer, then Codey and I hopped in the truck and took off. My brother-in-law and his friend followed us for a couple miles. Soon as their headlights disappeared from view, I turned the truck around to get that pitiful little deer out of the woods and into my truck bed. It may not have been the deer we wanted, but it was the deer we got, and it wouldn't go to waste.

As we drove home with that button buck, I knew Codey had my back—literally and figuratively.

Exhibit B: When Kelly and I started dating hot and heavy, I began attending her church, Heritage Fellowship. Every week after service, the pastor opened the altar to anyone needing prayer or wanting to pray for others.

One week, I took advantage of the opportunity and made my way to the front. I dropped to the stairs and bowed my head. A few minutes later, I finished praying and realized I'd gotten myself into a dilemma.

Getting to the front of the church was easy—there were plenty of things to grab onto for maintaining my balance. Standing up from the stairs was a different story. There were no pew arms or railings to help me to my feet. Distraught, I scanned the auditorium and made eye contact with Gracie. She smiled that big Gracie smile, then practically skipped down the aisle to help me to my feet.

Do your kids do this for you? Mine do.

Chapter 16

Uncovering the Butterfly

SINCE MY INJURY IN 2009, butterflies have shown up at a number of important moments. I now realize God used them to get my attention. Or He tried to use them to get my attention. The truth is that I didn't put much stock in the butterflies for a long time. Sure, I noticed them when the winged creatures crossed my path, but I didn't put any effort into infusing them with meaning. In 2010, God did what I was too dense to do on my own.

I wasn't back to work yet, but I was trying my best to get there, alternating between rehab at Siskin and self-guided workouts at the YMCA. Most of my day, however, was spent at home, resting after a hard rehab or workout session. I used some of that downtime to read the Bible.

On one such day, I flipped to Luke 8 and read the parable of the sower. I thanked God for transforming the soil of my heart so that it would accept His Word, then kept reading. In verse twenty-one, Jesus stated that His family members are those who hear and obey God's Word. I prayed that I would never hear God's Word without also doing what it requires. I continued reading about Jesus persuading His disciples to sail across the lake, only to fall asleep immediately after setting sail. An unexpected storm showed up and tossed the boat to and fro, but Jesus wasn't concerned. He kept sleeping. Freaking out, the disciples woke Jesus—hopefully not with a slap to the face. Jesus rubbed the sleep from his eyes and rebuked the waves and wind.

Following Jesus's rebuke, Luke writes five words: *and there was a calm.*

When I read those words, the Holy Spirit spoke to me. His voice wasn't audible and no clouds parted in the sky, but I heard Him clearly. *Mark*, he said, *do you remember when you were on the boat and saw the three butterflies?* I did. When they crossed my path, the screaming stopped. My breathing calmed, and my spirit followed suit. *Then there was one on the ceiling in the entryway at Memorial Hospital in Savannah.* Yes, I remember. *At the check-in desk at Shepherd Center.* I saw that. *Above your bed in your joint room with Eric, painted on the tile overhead.* Stared at it every day. *And printed on your mattress, the sheets, the nurse's scrubs and hair clip.*

Butterflies flitted through my memory, their translucent wings patting my shoulder.

Those were all for you, the Holy Spirit continued. *You needed calm in those moments, and I provided it.*

On the boat, I rotated between unconsciousness and uncontrollable screaming for four and one-half hours.

There were only three exceptions, three brief moments of peace. Each came on the wings of a butterfly.

And there was a calm . . .

I had you then, and I have you now, the Spirit spoke to my soul. *If I care for those tiny creatures that are here today and gone tomorrow, why would I not also care for you?*

Months after the first butterfly blessing, God opened my eyes. Suddenly, I saw His hand everywhere I looked. Granted, I should have seen it before. His mighty works were nothing new. In Numbers, a donkey talks. In Daniel, the ravenous lions kept their mouths closed. In Jonah, a giant fish protected a stubborn prophet from certain death. All these occurred because God, who created all things, is sovereign. And within His sovereign will, He found it fit to send a butterfly to one of His hurting children.

God didn't send those butterflies because I deserved His blessing and comfort. He sent them because He loves me. Through His Word, God restored my vision, and butterflies took on a new beauty. Beyond being a delicate, lovely part of creation, they became reminders of God's goodness.

————

Butterflies may not have such meaning for you. But if you love Jesus, there are butterflies in your life—reminders that despite the sin you commit against your Lord each day, He loves you. Your butterfly may be a spouse's smile or the tug of a bluegill on your fishing line. It may be a well-placed comma or the afghan your grandmother gave you last Christmas. Whatever your butterfly is, God gave it to you as a gift. See it for what it is, and give thanks.

I do. It took a while to see those butterflies properly, but thanks to God, I do now.

So, when I saw butterflies printed alongside Kelly's poem in *GoodNews*, I didn't hesitate. God had used butterflies for my good in the past. I trusted He was using them again, this time showing me it was safe to reach out to a stranger who knew hardship and hope. Then He used a Facebook message to once again change my life forever.

Those same butterflies have opened the door to share the Gospel. I give my testimony every opportunity I can, and the Nauti Dawg accident gives me more opportunity than I could have imagined. One opportunity was particularly special.

In late 2011, I returned to Savannah for vacation. While I was there, I wanted to meet Tommy, the firefighter who stabilized my neck and protected me from the elderly, slap-happy security guard after my accident.

I drove to the fire station closest to the marina where I met Tommy and rolled up to the front door in my wheelchair. A woman approached. I told her about my accident and that I wanted to thank the firefighter who helped me.

"Do you know who he is?" she asked.

"His name's Tommy," I said, "and he has a very authoritative voice. That's all I know."

The lady chuckled. She knew Tommy. Unfortunately, he'd been promoted to Lieutenant and wasn't at that station any more. "But if you leave a message," she said, "I'll have him call you."

The next night, my phone rang at ten o'clock. It was a Georgia phone number. I answered it on the second ring.

"Is this Mr. Wells?" A familiar voice called out from the other end of the phone. "This is Lt. Tommy Blackston with the Savannah Fire Department."

I confirmed that I was Mark Wells, and I wanted to thank him in person for helping me two years earlier.

"You were having a hard time that day, weren't you?" he said.

We talked a bit more, and then he told me he had another job. He was the pastor of a local church. I offered to give my testimony to his congregation sometime.

"You've got tomorrow's service," he said.

Tomorrow? That was Christmas day!

Flabbergasted, I accepted. The next morning, I told Lt. Blackston's congregation how God had worked in my life over the previous two years, starting my story with reggae music and the Nauti Dawg's shirtless captain. I detailed Lt. Pastor Blackston's good work and thanked Tommy again for keeping my unknown slapper at bay.

"The people of my church back home lifted me up in prayer, brought me food, and served me in ways I'll never know," I said near the end of my talk. "I don't understand how anybody makes it without a church family. To be honest, I don't think you can."

After the service, a man in his mid-twenties

approached. He thanked me for sharing my testimony, then shared a bit of his own. "I ran away when I was a little boy," he said. "I don't have any family—or didn't until today." My story convinced that runaway that he needed people. Specifically, he needed to join himself to a body of believers. That day, he became a member of Lt. Pastor Blackston's church.

My heart leapt at the news, knowing that another person would find their needs met through Christ's Church. Knowing that our sovereign God used someone as broken as me to bring another broken person into God's family—it's enough to bring even the most able-bodied to their knees.

If you have a story—and you do if you're one of God's children—share it. You don't know who needs to hear it or how God will use it. And if you aren't sure where your story begins and ends, look at the cross, where the author and finisher of our faith changed history and your story forever.

Chapter 17

The Story Continues

As I write this sentence, I'm in pain. As you read these words, I'm still in pain. Unless I'm dead, I'm in pain.

Years after my deep-sea misadventure, I hurt all day, every day. Nerve damage from the accident makes my feet feel like they're on fire at all times. I've learned to control my screaming impulse, but don't let that fool you. I'm hurting.

Since I can't fight or take flight, my fight-or-flight response is dead. Guess my brain dropped it to limit the stress I feel in stressful situations.

For years after my accident, I felt vulnerable sitting in a church auditorium if I didn't know who was behind me and what they were doing. I feared for my safety and sat at the back, so no one could sneak up behind me. This fear has dissolved a bit. I've learned to trust God more, to take Him at His word that He's taking care of me at all times.

That said, I've had to change some habits to protect against fear. One is cutting myself off from the news. I used to keep up with local and national news, but I can't any longer. Reports of school and church shootings bring fears to the surface, so I leave the TV off.

I've also gained an intimate knowledge of my limits. Since my landing on the Nauti Dawg, I'm no longer fooled into thinking I'm self-sufficient. I reach the end of myself moments after I wake up, and I rest my quality of life fully in the hands of God and those He puts in my path.

I'm still confused how the accident messed up my blood sugars, but I'm diabetic. I take my diabetes medication every day and wear a continuous glucose monitor on my triceps. If something feels off, I open an app on my phone to check my glucose numbers.

Every step I take requires extreme mental focus. *Raise the right foot, fling it forward, let it drop. Raise the left foot, fling it forward, let it drop.*

To top matters off, my routine is governed by my bathroom schedule. Every four hours, I empty my bladder via a catheter. I can wait a couple extra hours sometimes, and I go eight hours at night. But if I go longer than that, I risk some serious problems. Even when I empty on time, I get urinary tract infections. Since losing feeling below the waist, I've cathed myself 22,380 times with catheters that cost $100 a month after insurance pitches in. I'd rather not add up how much I've spent on catheters over the years.

My bowel situation isn't much better. If my brain decides not to release anything, I have no option but to wait it out with increasing stomach pains.

Along with snails, I've grown to dislike worms and squirrels.

Why worms? They wind up all over the sidewalk after it rains. That leaves me with a conundrum: get worm guts on the end of my cane or dodge the worms and wind up without the support I need to stay on my feet.

Why squirrels? When I first returned home from Shepherd Center, a feisty squirrel launched at me. I was in my wheelchair and fought it off, but not before the crazed thing shredded my face.*

On the plus side, I don't suffer from road rage anymore. At least not as often as I used to. There's not much I can do to someone who doesn't know how to drive, so there's no need to get upset.

Speaking of the plus side, Kelly and I remain happily married. The day after our honeymoon, we purchased ten acres in Riceville, Tennessee. A year and a half later, we moved into a ramshackle cabin on the property. Thankfully, Codey still lived at home and helped do a lot of repairs.

I also became friends with one of Kelly's old landlords, who was a retired homebuilder. When I told him my plans to build a second house on the east part of our new property, he came out of retirement to help us build. The whole family pitched in, digging footers, clearing out brush, and running electrical wire.

---

*Confession: The squirrel story didn't happen quite that way, but a squirrel did look at me like he wanted to attack me. So, I've put squirrels on my Naughty List.

In January of 2020, Kelly, Gracie, and I moved out of the cabin and into our new home. We left the cabin to Codey.

Within three years, Codey transformed the cabin into a warm, welcoming home. He replaced the flooring, moved some walls around, and refinished both bathrooms. Most importantly, he fell in love and married Lindsey, who loves their cabin. The couple bought forty more acres across the street and plan to build a new house there, surrounded by cow pasture.

Gracie is months away from graduating from Lee University with her elementary education degree. She's thrilled to follow in her mother's footsteps, and I can't wait to hear stories of children being blessed by Gracie's sweet spirit and can-do attitude. If you know Gracie, you know there will be lots of those stories coming.

———

Despite the joy I've experienced, my story involves a lot of suffering. The Scofield Bible helped me make sense of suffering a long time ago.

> *It must be confessed that beyond reasonable doubt, men cannot require a God who is sovereign to give explanation for what He chooses to do and not do.*

Instead of requiring God to explain His every move, I

should worship Him. It is the only fitting response.

I realize that a lot of people experience life-altering accidents. Many have had things go right also. So, why did I decide to write my story? Because my story is not my own. It belongs to my Creator, and I want to shout His story in every way possible.

I don't give my testimony to earn God's favor or repay God for all He's done for me, because there's nothing I can do to earn God's favor or repay Him. I give my testimony because I'm so thankful for and convicted by His goodness.

God knows I'm in pain. He could relieve me of that pain at any moment, and I believe that moment will come when my time here is finished. In the meantime, I trust God won't give me more than I can bear without a way of escape.

As a diabetic paraplegic, there's a lot I can't bear. But the love, patience, and assistance of family, friends, and the Holy Spirit offer a way of escape. So, I lean on those around me. And on days when I trick myself into thinking God has forgotten me, I look up for those butterflies that are always nearby.

www.ingramcontent.com/pod-product-compliance
Ingram Content Group UK Ltd.
Pitfield, Milton Keynes, MK11 3LW, UK
UKHW041037260325
456749UK00001B/20

9 798891 240957